THE ULTIMATE ACE DIET

Janette Marshall, an award-winning writer specializing in food and health, has been translating scientific findings about diet and health into practical ways of improving our well-being for the last ten years. Her last book, *The Eat for Life Diet* (Vermilion 1991, written with Anne Heughan) laid to rest the myth that experts can't agree on what constitutes healthy eating. A former editor of *BBC Good Health* magazine and deputy editor of *BBC Good Food*, she is a regular contributor to national newspapers and magazines. She lives in London and is secretary to the Guild of Food Writers.

THE
ULTIMATE
ACE
DIET

The antioxidant vitamins that help you live
longer, look younger and protect yourself
against major disease

Janette Marshall

VERMILION
LONDON

First published in 1994

1 3 5 7 9 10 8 6 4 2

First published in the United Kingdom in 1994 by Vermilion an imprint of Ebury Press Random House, 20 Vauxhall Bridge Road, London SW1V 2SA

Random House Australia (Pty) Limited 20 Alfred Street, Milsons Point, Sydney New South Wales 2061, Australia

Random House New Zealand Limited 18 Poland Road, Glenfield, Auckland 10, New Zealand

Random House South Africa (Pty) Limited PO Box 337, Bergvlei, South Africa

Random House UK Limited Reg. No. 954009

A CIP catalogue record for this book is available from the British Library

ISBN 0 09 178342 9

Printed and bound in Great Britain by Mackays of Chatham plc, Chatham, Kent

This book gives non-specific, general advice and should not be relied on as a substitute for proper medical consultation. The author and publisher cannot accept responsibility for illness arising out of the failure to seek medical advice from a doctor.

Contents

ACKNOWLEDGEMENTS

To all the scientists researching to increase our knowledge of antioxidants and how to improve our health through diet.

Thanks to Wendy Doyle for analysing the recipes and to Wendy, Dr Martin Wiseman and Anne Heughan for constructive comments on the text.

To Lydia Sidaway for recipe-testing and valuable comments.

To my agent Mark Lucas.

Introduction

By now most people are aware of the big healthy eating messages (even if they don't follow them). These messages are: cut down on fat; eat lots of foods rich in starch and fibre; don't eat sugary foods too often.

This is sound advice if you want to avoid coronary heart disease, cancer and weight problems. But how many people are aware of the 'twiddly bits' of their diet – the additional little things that make as great a contribution to well-being as eating less fatty food (especially saturated fat) and more starchy food such as bread, potatoes, pasta, rice and vegetables? Not many, it seems, because those 'twiddly bits' – the ACE nutrients – are found mainly in fruit and vegetables and, as *The Ultimate ACE Diet* shows, most people don't eat nearly enough of them.

But first things first. Why call this book *The Ultimate ACE Diet?* ACE stands for vitamins A, C and E, and this book is about why we need to eat more of them to be healthy. However, it could equally well have been called *The Antioxidant Diet*, or *5-a-Day for the UK*. Someone even suggested *The Free-radical Buster (Diet) Book* (for reasons that will become apparent later).

The trouble with those optional titles is that not many people are familiar as yet with terms like 'antioxidant' and 'free radical'. And there was an additional difficulty with the title *5-a-Day for the UK* – the people we tried it on were not sure whether it meant they should eat five meals a day. Or only five types of food a day. Or the same food five times. There were even those who thought it meant you made love five times a day in order to lose weight! In fact, *5-a-Day for the UK* refers to five portions of fruit and/or vegetables a day (including nuts, seeds and pulses) – roughly the amount you need to eat to ensure there are enough ACE vitamins and minerals in your diet to protect you.

If you are thinking, 'I suppose this means the experts have changed their minds yet again about what constitutes a healthy diet,' you are wrong. The discovery of the importance of ACE nutrients is confirmation of worldwide consensus about what constitutes a healthy diet. It builds on and clarifies earlier findings and points the way ahead. It is also relevant to everyone because all of us – men, women and children, old and young – need ACE nutrients. Many of us are probably not eating enough, and without them we may be exposing ourselves unnecessarily to an increased risk of coronary heart disease and cancer.

The good news is that with the practical help and advice in this book – including more than 70 tried-and-tested recipes rich in ACE nutrients – you can do something positive to improve your health and that of your family. And it's not just me saying so. *The Health Survey for England 1991*, published in 1993, shows that no one can be complacent about diet and lifestyle. It reveals, for example:

- Only 12 per cent of men and 11 per cent of women have none of the four main risk factors for heart disease and stroke (smoking, raised blood pressure, raised cholesterol, lack of physical activity).
- The proportion of obese (very overweight) adults has increased since 1986 from 7 to 13 per cent for men and from 12 to 15 per cent for women.
- Sixteen per cent of men and 17 per cent of women have high blood pressure and most are not taking any medication to lower it.
- Only 20 per cent of men and 12 per cent of women do enough exercise.

It is not surprising, therefore, that the government has formed a Nutrition Task Force whose job it is to find ways of helping us to reduce the amount and change the type of fat we eat, avoid obesity and, as a result of those changes, bring down high blood pressure. This follows the government's Health of the Nation strategy, which set targets to reduce premature death and disabling disease by the year 2000. And this is where the *The Ultimate ACE Diet* comes in, for it contains the basics of a health plan that will take you to the year 2000 and beyond.

Janette Marshall, 1994

CHAPTER 1

How The Ultimate ACE Diet Can Help You

Whether you live to eat or eat to live, the food you choose affects the way you look and feel. As children we all learn that it's necessary to eat up in order to grow up big and strong, but it has only recently been discovered that some foods are also good at protecting us against disease. Experts now believe that antioxidant vitamins and minerals – or ACE nutrients – can protect against cancer and coronary heart disease, two of the most devastating diet-related diseases known to man, and maybe influence other ailments too.

What are antioxidant nutrients?

Vitamin A, in the form of **beta carotene** (the yellow, orange and red pigment found mainly in fruit and vegetables), is an antioxidant. Beta carotene is also a pro-vitamin, which means it is turned into vitamin A in the body. There are lots of other carotenes that are antioxidants and some are also pro-vitamins.

Vitamin C is an antioxidant found in fruit and vegetables, the best source being citrus fruit.

Vitamin E is an antioxidant found in nuts, seeds and vegetable oils and products made from them.

Beta carotene, other carotenes and vitamin C are found in combination in most orange fruit and vegetables, and they also occur in other vegetables, particularly dark green ones (where the colour is masked by the stronger green chlorophyll colouring).

Food also contains antioxidant minerals such as **selenium**, **zinc**, **copper** and **manganese**.

Who says we need them?

While many scientists are already convinced that we should eat more foods rich in ACE nutrients, such as fruit and vegetables, scores of research projects testing this theory have yet to be completed. In Britain, the Ministry of Agriculture, Fisheries and Food is spending more than £2m on research into ACE nutrients. A Department of Health COMA (Committee on Medical Aspects of Food Policy) working group on Diet and Cancer is reviewing the evidence on antioxidants so they can tell us how to eat to avoid cancer. But they won't report until 1996 and some of the research will take even longer.

However, *you can act now* on the initial findings (which are very substantial and persuasive), and in so doing you will benefit yourself and your family – for, even though there is still more to learn about ACE nutrients, there is enough information available to enable you to improve health and well-being.

Even if you don't think you are at risk from coronary heart disease, cancer or the many diet-related diseases that are a problem for the UK today – strokes, high blood pressure, obesity, diabetes, bowel problems, gallstones, tooth decay, osteoporosis – prevention is always worth considering, especially as several of these are 'silent' diseases and you might not know you have them until they are already well established.

While you might say, 'That's OK by me, I'd rather die young and happy than deny myself the pleasures of life,' in reality you don't have to make such a stark choice. You *can* have it both ways. In other words, the changes to diet and lifestyle may need only be small and they can be enjoyable.

This is especially worth considering when you know that not every heart attack is a painless and quick way to go! They don't all occur on the golf course, or at the height of whatever is your particular ecstasy. And some of the other diseases against which ACE nutrients can protect can be disabling and painful for a long time.

But let's not look on the black side. Suffice it to say that if you want to, you can help yourself to a longer, healthier, more active and more enjoyable life, and it won't hurt a bit.

From the studies already done it's known that people who eat too little fruit and vegetables have a greater risk of cancer and heart disease than people who eat a good amount. But apart from preventing those two diseases, ACE nutrients can also help in lots of other areas of your life. For example, studies are continuing right now into how they might:

- Boost your immunity, which could give you better protection against a whole host of conditions from the common cold upwards.
- Slow down the ageing process that leads to wrinkles, skin blemishes and general decay and decrepitude.
- Protect against cataracts and possibly macular degeneration, the two commonest causes of loss of sight as we age.
- Improve the quality of men's sperm (which has, apparently, been deteriorating over the last 50 years).
- Improve lung function and thereby fitness potential.
- Help prevent or treat arthritis.

Why you should take the ACE pledge

The list above could be longer, but for now it serves to make the point that you would do well to eat more foods rich in ACE nutrients on a daily basis. So if you act only on one piece of information in this book make it this one, and take the ACE Pledge:

From today I am going to eat five or more portions of fruit and/or vegetables a day.

This adds up to around 400g/14oz a day, excluding potatoes and other starchy vegetables, and including about 30g/1oz of pulses, nuts and seeds. A lot of the evidence for this advice comes from studies of people living in Mediterranean countries who follow their traditional diet and lifestyle and enjoy longer – and healthier – lives than northern Europeans and North Americans.

Until recently it was thought they gained their protection solely from eating less fat (especially saturated animal fat), which meant they had lower blood cholesterol levels. However, it has been discovered that it is not quite that simple. The differences in fat alone failed to explain differing rates of coronary heart disease (although the advice is still to eat less fat, especially saturated fat). Certainly a high-fat diet does account for a lot of fat people living in the Mediterranean! But it doesn't seem to make those who eat a traditional Mediterranean diet more likely to have coronary heart disease, or some cancers.

What probably makes the real difference is the amount of fruit and vegetables eaten and the *type* of fat, which is usually extra-virgin olive oil, containing vitamin E. So, even if a high-fat diet is eaten, the ACE nutrients in fruit, vegetables and olive oil are giving protection. The way they do this is covered in more detail later, but a simple explanation is that the antioxidants in fruit and vegetables prevent cholesterol in the blood from narrowing and hardening the arteries, the process that leads to a heart attack. Similarly, ACE nutrients can also prevent chemical changes in the body that lead to certain types of cancer.

By studying the diet of different populations and the amount and type of disease they suffer, scientists so far haven't been able to prove cause and effect between low levels of ACE nutrients and disease, but they have shown us that there's a strong association.

What are the recommendations?

The initial suggestion of the value of ACE nutrients goes back about 30 years, when scientists first made a link between low levels of the ACE nutrient beta carotene and increased risk of cancer. It was proposed that if you ate more beta carotene-rich foods you reduced your cancer risk, possibly due to the antioxidant activity of beta carotene.

Since then there has been a huge amount of scientific research on the effects of antioxidants on different types of cancer, coronary heart disease and other diseases, and all of it has come to similar conclusions: that people with a high fruit and vegetable intake halve their risk of cancer and heart disease compared with those who eat little fruit and vegetables. These findings have led to the following recommendations.

The World Health Organisation recommends that we eat 400g/14oz of fruit and vegetables a day (the current average is around 200g/7oz). The WHO report *Diet, Nutrition and the Prevention of Chronic Diseases* (1990) says that vegetables and fruit are a rich source of vitamins, minerals and fibre and are low in calories. And although no one has yet worked out how many grams of each vitamin and mineral each individual needs to eat to prevent different diseases, there is convincing evidence that vegetables and fruit play a protective role in preventing certain cancers. Whether it is the ACE nutrients or some other as yet unknown substance(s) that prevent disease is not yet clear. The report concludes that people living in countries with a low incidence of coronary heart disease, certain types of cancer, high blood pressure and some diabetes (such as those in the Mediterranean region), eat around 400g/14oz a day of vegetables (not including potatoes) and fruit, including about 30g/1oz of pulses, nuts and seeds – all good sources of ACE nutrients. And they obtain a lot of vitamin E from vegetable oils.

Diet and Cancer (1989, published by the Health Education Authority [HEA] for Europe Against Cancer) said diets containing a variety of fruit and vegetables may protect against cancers of the lung, large bowel, oesophagus and stomach. It therefore recommends that we eat more fruit and vegetables, especially raw and lightly cooked green vegetables and salads.

Eight Guidelines for a Healthy Diet (1990, published by the Ministry of Agriculture, Fisheries and Food, the Department of Health and the HEA) recommends eating more fruit and vegetables on a daily basis.

Dietary Reference Values for Food Energy and Nutrients for the UK (the report drawn up by the Department of Health in 1991 stating how many calories, vitamins and minerals are essential to health) recommends eating more bread, potatoes, rice, pasta, fruit and vegetables at the expense of foods rich in saturated fat and added sugars (i.e. full-fat dairy produce, fatty meat and meat products, chocolate, biscuits, cakes, pastry, margarine). So the largest proportion of food on the plate would be starchy fibre-rich food and fruit and vegetables.

The government has also commissioned research to investigate the importance of ACE nutrients. The Ministry of Agriculture,

Fisheries and Food (MAFF) is now funding nine antioxidant research projects into how these nutrients might help prevent heart disease, cancer and rheumatoid arthritis.

The areas scientists are working on include:

- Improving the knowledge of how antioxidants work in the body.
- Exploring the role of free radicals (more about these in Chapter 2) and how they might cause diseases such as heart disease and cancer.
- Developing a better understanding of how body cells and tissues are protected from free-radical damage.
- Trying to find out the optimum intakes of antioxidant vitamins and minerals (i.e. the amounts needed to prevent disease) so that they can be used in trials.
- Trying to establish if some of us have greater needs for vitamins, and other antioxidant nutrients, than others. (It's already known, for instance, that smokers need more vitamin C.)
- Considering whether food needs to be fortified with antioxidant nutrients (in the same way that white bread and margarine are fortified with vitamins and minerals).

The Consumers' Association studied 100 international government-approved reports published between 1961 and 1991 and found that 65 specifically advised eating more fruit and vegetables. An additional six advised eating more vegetables.

In America, *Diet & Health*, published in 1989 by the US National Research Council, gave the advice: 'Every day eat five or more servings of a combination of vegetables and fruit, especially green and yellow vegetables and citrus fruit . . . diets high in plant food – i.e. fruit, vegetables, legumes and whole grain cereals – are associated with a lower occurrence of coronary heart disease and cancer of the lung, colon, oesophagus and stomach.'

5-A-Day for Better Health, an American government campaign with the American National Cancer Institute and the Produce for Better Health Foundation also advises eating five daily portions of fruit and vegetables, while the National Academy of Sciences recommends:

- Every day eat five or more servings of a combination of vegetables and fruit, especially green and yellow vegetables and citrus fruit.
- Green and yellow vegetables to emphasize in the diet include carrots, broccoli, winter squash, spinach, kale, greens. These vegetables are the richest sources of beta carotene.
- Citrus fruit to emphasize in the diet include oranges, tangerines, and grapefruit. These are excellent sources of vitamin C.
- For maximum nutrient retention, vegetables should be cooked in minimal amounts of water and only until they reach the tender but still crisp stage. Cooking this way helps to retain the vitamin C content of vegetables.
- Because a certain amount of vitamin C is lost even in brief, careful cooking, some vegetables and fruit should be consumed in their fresh, raw state.

Health patterns in the UK

In the UK, deaths from heart disease are mirrored by the consumption patterns of fruit and vegetables. There are more deaths in Scotland, Northern Ireland and the north of England, where consumption of these foods is lowest. Heart disease is also highest in lower social classes which have a lower consumption of fruit and vegetables. The consumption of wholemeal and brown bread (some of which contains wheatgerm, a rich source of vitamin E) and cereal products is lower in the lower social classes. (see Table 1, page 18).

Reference Nutrient Intake

An RNI, set by the British Government, is the amount that is enough of a particular vitamin or mineral for virtually everyone, including those with high requirements. The RNI is higher than most people need, so anyone eating that much of an nutrient is unlikely to be deficient. (More about RNIs and other Dietary Reference Values in Appendix 1, page 181)

Table 1: Regional differences in antioxidant nutrient content of British Household Food (1992)

Region	Vitamin A (micrograms per day)	Beta carotene (micrograms per day)	Vitamin C (milligrams per day)
Scotland	780	1,670	50
Wales	820	1,870	48
England	870	1,750	51
Regions of England:			
North	790	1820	47
Yorkshire & Humberside	900	1,800	49
North West	850	1,670	46
East Midlands	810	1,780	49
West Midlands	880	1,610	44
South West	830	1,780	53
South East & Anglia	920	1,770	56

Ministry of Agriculture Fisheries and Food, Household Food Consumption and Expenditure 1992.

Table 2: Average daily vitamin E (mg) intake from all sources

Regions of Britain	Men	Women
Scotland	10	7.7
Northern	11.5	7.7
Central, South West and Wales	11.9	8.5
London and South East	12	9.7

The Dietary and Nutrition Survey of British Adults (16–64) 1990.

18

Table 3: Regional differences in antioxidant nutrient content of diet as a percentage of reference nutrient intake (RNI) (1992)

Region	Vitamin A	Vitamin C
Scotland	171	131
Wales	182	124
England	187	133

Ministry of Agriculture Fisheries and Food, Household Food Consumption and Expenditure 1992. No figures available for vitamin E.

Do you eat enough fruit and vegetables?

The following tables give an idea of the variation between regions of the UK in the amount of fruit and vegetables eaten. Consumption of fresh green leafy salads, for example, is 18 per cent higher than average in the South East and 25 per cent lower than average in northern households. People in Yorkshire, Humberside and the North West eat about 8 per cent less salad than average. The same is true for cabbage and brussels sprouts, while the Scots consume 50 per cent fewer brussels sprouts than the national average and 35 per cent less cabbage.

As you would expect from that, more (3 per cent) is spent on fruit and vegetables in the South than any other region: Wales spends 11 per cent less than the national average and Scotland 12 per cent less.

Ten per cent less fruit than average is eaten in Scotland and Wales and 4 per cent above average in England. Oranges are the only fruit eaten more in the North (8 per cent) than the South. In general, households in Wales and the West Midlands eat less fruit and drink less fruit juice than the rest of the country.

The above statistics, dating from 1991, are a continuation of a longer-term trend. Between 1977 and 1991 the South East and East Anglia have consumed 20 per cent more fruit than the rest of the population. And as you can see from the table overleaf, intakes of the ACE nutrient beta carotene have fallen, although vitamin C intake has risen (except in Wales and the North West).

19

Table 4: Nutritional Value of Household Food, National Averages 1989-1992

	1989	1990	1991	1992
Beta-carotene micrograms per day	2,440	1,880	1,910	1,750
Vitamin C milligrams per day	54	52	55	51
Vitamin E milligrams per day	*	*	*	8.1

* = Vitamin E figures not available.

Ministry of Agriculture Fisheries and Food, Household Food Consumption and Expenditure 1992.

According to a survey of British lifestyle by the Co-op, in general we are eating more fruit and fewer vegetables (see Table 5). This trend is not good news because it's likely that vegetables may be

Table 5: Changes in fruit and vegetable consumption over the past decade (ounces per person per week)

Region	Fruit 1979	Fruit 1989	Veg 1979	Veg 1989
UK	28.06	32.40	85.37	82.01
Scotland	24.55	26.72	76.54	84.18
Wales	29.36	28.37	98.31	85.37
England	28.36	33.29	85.60	81.55
North	21.50	28.95	89.50	87.67
Midlands	25.20	31.20	84.60	84.65
North West	24.30	31.20	84.80	78.73
South West	27.85	37.00	86.79	84.04
SouthEast/Anglia	34.65	39.36	84.11	76.92
% changes		+13.50		-8.50

Table 6: Vegetables: Number of ounces eaten at home per person per week

	1980	1989
Total	85.37	82.01
Potatoes	41.00	35.59
Fresh green vegetables	12.40	10.20
Total processed vegetables	16.17	19.06

Table 7: Fruit – Number of ounces eaten at home per person per week

	1980	1989
Total	28.06	32.40
Fresh fruit	20.81	21.45
Canned fruit	1.79	2.15
Fruit juices	3.08	7.52

slightly more protective than fruit – although both are important. While the South might seem to be doing a little better than the North there is no room for complacency, because compared with our European neighbours, for example Italy and France (see page 49), we could all do a lot better.

Vitamins

According to a survey of the diet and nutrition of British adults completed in 1987, most people were getting enough vitamins from their diet to prevent deficiency diseases (e.g. scurvy) but probably not enough for so-called optimal health – a state associated with low incidence of coronary heart disease, cancer and other diseases. In general, older people had higher intakes of vitamins from food, especially vitamin A and some of the B vitamins – perhaps an indication that they cook more fresh food, especially vegetables. Women in the 16–24 and 25–34 age groups consistently ate a diet that provided fewer of these essential nutrients (which is particularly worrying, as this is the age that most women have children and there is growing evidence that future health depends on nutrition in the uterus). Lower intakes among younger women were not due to slimming: slimmers in the survey had good intakes of vitamins, many of them taking supplements. Vegetables provided 70 per cent of beta carotene and 46 per cent of vitamin C. Twenty-two per cent of vitamin C came from drinks and 17 per cent from fruit.

Women aged 16–24 and 25–34 also had significantly lower intakes of vitamin C, although they did eat 30mg/day, enough to prevent deficiencies; however, the government has since raised the RNI figure to 40mg/day. But this may not be enough for optimal health.

It's a similar story for vitamin E. Women in the 35–49 age group had the highest intakes and women aged 16–24 were significantly below average.

Minerals

The same survey showed that women under 50 and men aged 16–24 were not getting enough iron from their diet to meet RDA needs (Recommended Daily Amounts of nutrients, which have since been replaced by Dietary Reference Values, see page 15 and Appendix 1, page 181). However, women were well above the required amount of calcium. At the time, these were the only two minerals with UK RDAs. Cereal products, including bread which is fortified, provided the highest proportion of iron (42 per cent). Meat, which most people think of as the main provider of iron, supplied 23 per cent and meat products 15 per cent. However, the iron in meat is much better absorbed.

Once again, the trend was for younger people to have lower intakes of minerals from their diet than older people. As well as being short of iron, men under 25 and women under 35 had lower than average intakes of copper and zinc (both ACE nutrients).

Children's eating habits do not seem to be improving. According to a report by the ASDA supermarket chain, 19 per cent of all children refuse to try new foods and do not eat the same food as their parents. They eat snack foods rather than balanced meals. A further 15 per cent of children are classified as 'junk food fiends'. Only 32 per cent of children are considered to eat a well-adjusted diet and accept what they are given.

The same survey showed that in families where children wouldn't eat particular foods those families did not buy them, resulting in consumption of green vegetables 25 per cent below average (20 per cent for salads) with 40 per cent of children over-all disliking greens and 30 per cent disliking salad.

What quantity of ACE nutrients do YOU need?

While we have seen that governments and other bodies are able to recommend that we eat more fruit and vegetables and other foods rich in ACE nutrients, they have not yet managed to find the answer to the 64-million-dollar question – how much of each ACE nutrient does each individual need to prevent heart disease, cancer and other health problems?

The answer to this is one that will take scientists, governments and their advisory panels decades to decide. The delay is in part because it takes so long to do 'intervention' trials. In these trials large groups of people are given vitamin pills over periods as long as ten years to see whether or not ACE nutrients can prevent disease and what is the best dose (see Chapter 3).

Meanwhile, you know there are advantages in eating more fruit and vegetables that contain ACE nutrients and it's understandable that you don't want to wait. You want to act now to protect yourself and your family. So what do you do next?

1. To take the ACE Pledge (page 13) and increase the amount of ACE vitamins and minerals that you and your family eat with the aim of improving your health and protecting yourself against disease, turn to Chapters 4 and 5.
2. To discover the exact amount of ACE vitamins and minerals recommended by the British government, and what foods they are in, turn to Appendix I (page 181).
3. To find out how ACE nutrients protect your health, turn to Chapter 2.

CHAPTER 2

What Are Antioxidants, and How Do They Work?

The main antioxidant nutrients are beta carotene, vitamins C and E and the minerals selenium, zinc, manganese and copper. While these are the centre of much current research, there are also other substances that act as antioxidants and they may prove to be just as important (see pages 29–36). Antioxidant nutrients work together to destroy free radicals (and they may also work with other substances in food that are yet to be discovered).

What are free radicals?

Free radicals are highly reactive molecules that contain one or more 'free' electrons (electrons are usually paired). These free electrons grab electrons from another molecule, forming free-radical compounds which are potentially dangerous to the body. The process also disturbs the chemical balance by making another single unit and setting up a chain reaction leading to the production of more free radicals.

There's no escape from free radicals because they are a by-product of breathing oxygen and burning food to produce energy to live and work. Free radicals are also produced by cigarette smoke, car exhaust fumes and other pollutants, radiation from the sun, some drugs and pesticides.

If the level of free radicals is in balance with the ACE nutrients needed to control them then there is no problem, but if antioxidant levels are too low (i.e. you are not eating enough of the right ACE foods) then free radicals attack the body. They are thought to initiate heart disease by changing cholesterol to allow it to fur up arteries, and to cause cancers by destroying or altering the DNA (genetic material) in our cells.

Free radicals are not always harmful – for example, germ-killing cells called phagocytes use free radicals to kill bacteria. However, in many other instances, free radicals are more damaging than helpful. There are at least 50 diseases in which free radicals are possibly implicated.

The chemistry of fighting free radicals

The body has evolved a complex system to protect itself against free-radical (or oxidative) damage. Enzymes deactivate free radicals and antioxidants stabilize them. The enzyme superoxide dismutase (SOD for short – easy to remember) removes the superoxide radical, generated in profusion by normal cell functions and very dangerous because in the presence of stray copper and iron it is capable of turning into hydroxyl radical, the most damaging of all free radicals. In removing the superoxide radical SOD makes hydrogen peroxide and oxygen; the toxic hydrogen peroxide is then removed by two other enzymes called catalase and glutathione peroxidase.

Some antioxidants, such as uric acid, are produced in the body, but most of them are nutrients (vitamins and minerals) that cannot be made in the body and must be eaten.

Glutathione is made in the body from three amino acids (glutamate, cysteine and glycine) found in protein foods. In general, dairy products, bread and cereals are low in glutathione. Fresh meat is high and fruits and vegetables contain moderate amounts. Food processing (except freezing) decreases glutathione content. Researchers who have compiled data on the glutathione content of common foods think that the difference between the content of fresh and processed (mainly canned) fruit and vegetables is significant enough to suggest that people who do not eat much fresh food might be deficient in this antioxidant nutrient which is an important component of an antioxidant enzyme. In short, the system that defends the body against free radicals depends on a good supply of antioxidant vitains and minerals. These are as follows:

Antioxidant vitamins

Beta carotene

This is the pigment that gives yellow, orange and red fruit and vegetables their colour. It is also found in dark green leafy vegetables. It is a vitamin A precursor or pro-vitamin A, which means that it can be turned into vitamin A in the body as well as fulfilling its antioxidant role as beta carotene. Beta carotene is also present in the blood. As an antioxidant it works inside the cells of the body, where it can trap and destroy free radicals and singlet oxygen (an active form of oxygen that can lead to free-radical formation and may also be generated by free-radical reactions). This prevents damage to genetic material which might initiate cancer. Other types of carotenoid may also act as antioxidants, and their special areas of activity are being studied.

Vitamin C

This is found in fruit and vegetables – mainly citrus fruits and green leafy vegetables, though potatoes are a rich source in the British diet because we eat such a lot of them. It is a water-soluble vitamin and is the most potent antioxidant working in the watery parts of cells and in the fluid in which all cells are bathed.

Vitamin C scavenges free radicals. It is also thought to help regenerate vitamin E after the latter has neutralized free radicals. This allows vitamin E to return to its original state and fight free radicals for longer.

Vitamin E

Vitamin E is found in vegetable oils, nuts, wholemeal bread and cereals, eggs, margarine, sunflower spread, dairy produce and some fruit and green leafy vegetables. It is a fat-soluble vitamin and is the main antioxidant in the fatty parts of cells where it prevents oxidation of polyunsaturtates in the cell walls and interacts with particles of harmful cholesterol. If there is enough vitamin E in your body free radicals may be prevented from oxidizing cholesterol and causing damage to arterial walls. Vitamin E inhibits lipid (dietary fat) peroxidation chain reaction by combining with the oxygen free radical, preventing it from combining with the next fatty acid in the chain.

Vitamin E protects polyunsaturated fats (in vegetable oils, margarines and spreads) against oxidation (the process in which free radicals attack them and turn them into harmful substances) and also seems to protect beta carotene from being oxidized. Vitamin E, like other ACE nutrients, is especially valuable because it breaks down into harmless waste materials after it has done its work.

To be most effective, vitamin E needs vitamin C (see page 26).

Vitamin A

Vitamin A is not, strictly speaking, an antioxidant (except in the form of beta carotene, see page 26) but it does have some antioxidant characteristics. For example, it can scavenge singlet oxygen which is involved in free-radical damage. It also enhances the body's immune system, giving protection against disease, and helps control cell differentiation (cancer is a loss of control over cell differentiation).

Antioxidant minerals

Copper

Copper is a component of superoxide dismutase. It is needed to make caeruloplasmin, a substance that converts ferrous iron into ferric iron. By doing this it stops the ferrous iron being available to produce harmful free radicals.

Manganese

Manganese is a component of superoxide dismutase that works in a specific part of the cell called the mitochondria, where all the energy reactions take place.

Selenium

Selenium is a component of glutathione peroxidase which removes toxic by-products made when free radicals are destroyed by antioxidants.

Zinc

Zinc is also a component of superoxide dismutase and works inside cells breaking down free radicals.

Table 8: Good sources of antioxidant nutrients	
	Food sources
Minerals:	
Zinc	Meat, milk and milk products, bread, cereal, cereal products
Manganese	Wholegrain cereals, nuts, tea
Selenium	Cereals, especially bread, fish, liver, pork, cheese, eggs, walnuts, brazil nuts
Copper	Wholegrain cereals, meat, vegetables
Vitamins:	
Beta carotene	Yellow and orange fruits, particularly carrots, broccoli, tomatoes, melons, mangoes, apricots, peaches, pumpkin, watercress, prunes
Vitamin C	Fruit and vegetables, particularly citrus fruit, blackcurrants, strawberries, kiwifruits, gooseberries, guava, green leafy vegetables, peppers, potatoes, swede, parsnips
Vitamin E	Vegetable oils, particularly sunflower seed oils and products made from them, almonds, brazils, hazelnuts, wholegrain breakfast cereal, wholemeal bread, dark green vegetables, wheatgerm. Fruit and vegetables are not very good sources, but the best are apples, bananas, blackcurrants, damsons, asparagus, broccoli, carrots, peas, spinach, parsley, purslane, tomatoes, lettuce, watercress. A little is found in scallops and clams and some oily fish: mackerel, salmon
Vitamin A	Liver, kidney, dairy products, oily fish, fortified margarine.

Other sources of antioxidants

While those vitamins and minerals listed above are the main ACE nutrients, antioxidants have also been found in many other foods. In some they are not present in large enough amounts to be useful, while others are eaten only very infrequently in the British diet. However, they may provide scientists with natural sources of antioxidants to extract for use in future medicines or even food additives.

Some of these sources are:

Spices: Coriander, cloves, black pepper, turmeric, paprika, mustard powder.
Herbs: Sage, rosemary.
Vegetables: Onions.
Meat: Smoked and cured meat (because of the antioxidant food additives used in its production).
Fermented foods: Tempeh, miso.
Oilseed: Soya bean, sesame seed, peanut.
Others: Grape seeds, green tea.

How antioxidants help prevent heart disease

Heart disease is still the main killer in Britain, with 175,000 people dying of it each year. Many others are disabled by it.

Until recently it was thought that the main cause of heart disease was eating too much saturated fat, the effect of which is to raise blood cholesterol levels which in turn narrow arteries, increasing the risk of heart disease. But in fact it is an interaction of risk factors, including eating too much (saturated) fat, smoking, high blood pressure and lack of exercise. The role of ACE nutrients – antioxidants – explains things previously left a mystery by the lipid (dietary fat) hypothesis. To cite a few:

- Very low coronary heart disease (CHD) in countries like France, despite their comparatively high saturated fat intake.
- The different incidence of CHD between the social classes.
- A possible explanation of the greater risk of CHD in men than women.
- And partially why there is a greater risk in women after the menopause (see page 103).

As scientists re-examined the evidence, some missing parts of the jigsaw began to fall into place to reveal the importance of antioxidants.

1 Damage to artery walls usually has to happen before cholesterol can build up, narrow the arteries and so increase the risk of a heart attack. Antioxidants protect against this initial damage.
2 There are two types of cholesterol: the good type, HDL (high density lipoprotein), and the bad, LDL (low density lipoprotein). For LDL to accumulate and silt up the arteries it has first to be changed through a process called oxidation. (This is similar to the oxidation involved when butter goes rancid after being exposed to oxygen free radicals.)
3 This modification of LDL is thought to occur locally, i.e. at the site of damage to an artery wall. Oxidized LDL seems to promote the build-up of fatty plaque in the walls of the arteries. Exactly what triggers the damage to the artery wall in the first place and the oxidation of the LDL remains to be discovered. However, antioxidant nutrients can *prevent* oxidation of LDL.

The big question is: can they therefore prevent heart disease (along with a low-fat diet, adequate exercise and not smoking)? The evidence that they might be able to is accumulating, in particular through the link with fruit and vegetables. In Britain there are more incidences of heart disease in areas where consumption of these foods is lowest.

How antioxidants help prevent cancer

In Britain, 160,000 people die each year from cancer – the commonest cause of death after heart disease. About one in three cases of cancer is linked to food. Your diet can initiate cancer, promote it or prevent it.

As we have seen, low levels of beta carotene were associated with increased risk of cancer more than ten years ago. At the launch of the EPIC trial – the world's largest prospective survey of diet and cancer – in 1992, the scientists involved estimated that a huge number of deaths from cancer – about 40,000 a year in England and Wales – could be prevented by a change in diet.

Table 9: Cancer deaths possibly avoided by dietary change in England and Wales

Types of cancer	%	Number
Lung	20	6,916
Large bowel	90	15,153
Breast	50	7,004
Stomach	90	8,156
Prostate	10	785
Pancreas	50	3,058
Oesophagus	20	1,002
Bladder	20	950

From Table 10, page 32, you can see that fruit and vegetables are protective. However, it's not yet known whether the effects of fruit and vegetables on cancer development are due to their provision of ACE nutrients, or whether other components of these foods (see below) also exert powerful effects in preventing cancer or stopping pre-cancerous lesions developing into fully-fledged cancer.

What other antioxidants might protect you?

Apart from foods rich in ACE nutrients there are also other antioxidant substances, both in food and produced within the body, that can help to prevent free radical damage.

Antioxidant enzymes

The body makes these from minerals such as selenium, copper, manganese and zinc and uses them to block chemically induced cancers and inactivate free radicals. Consequently, a diet low in minerals can lower your defences.

Table 10: Summary of associations between diet and cancer

Site of cancer	Fat weight	Body	Fibre	Fruit and veg	Alcohol	Smoked, salted, pickled foods
Lung			−			
Breast	+	+			+/−	
Colon	++		−	−		
Prostate	++			−		
Bladder				−		
Rectum	+			−	+	
Endometrium		++				
Oral cavity				−	+[a]	
Stomach				−		++
Cervix				−		
Oesophagus				−	++[a]	+

+ Positive association: the more you eat the more likely you are to get cancer. Body weight: Breast and endometrial cancer are associated with excess weight.

− Negative association: the more you eat the less likely you are to get cancer

[a] Synergistic with smoking.

Caffeic and ferrulic acids

These are substances in plants that can block chemical changes that lead to cancer. They work in a similar way to the antioxidant vitamins C and E.

Chemopreventors

These are chemicals found in vegetables that stimulate production of enzymes that can detoxify carcinogens (cancer-causing agents).

Fibre

Fibre protects against large bowel cancer and may be more useful in preventing this disease than antioxidants. In a study of more than 7,000 male health professionals, those who had the highest-fibre diet had the lowest pre-cancerous growths in the colon and rectum. Antioxidant intake didn't alter their risk status. Fibre from starchy food ferments with gut bacteria to produce butyrate, a substance that slows down cell proliferation and therefore protects against cancer. Starchy fibre also leads to faster transit time and dilution of wastes in the gut. A high-fibre diet might also counteract the harmful effects of oestrogens in hormone-reliant cancers.

Flavonoids

Flavonoids are found in tea (especially green tea), onions and wine. They may act as antioxidants.

Folate

Folate (folic acid) is a member of the B vitamin family and is found in dark green leafy vegetables and cereals. It is thought to protect cells in a pre-cancerous condition by producing substances that can repair free-radical damage.

Garlic and onions

These contain allicin, a sulphur compound that induces production of substances that stimulate antioxidant mechanisms. In trials garlic has had beneficial effects on blood fats and blood pressure and has made blood less likely to clot (and cause a heart attack). Huge amounts of fresh garlic – a bulb or two a day – might be needed to obtain these effects; trials use garlic pills.

Lycopenes

This is another type of antioxidant carotene, responsible for the red colour of tomatoes. It is interesting because huge quantities of tomatoes are eaten in a traditional Mediterranean diet.

Phytates

Phytates are found in beans and cereals. These substances can bind with minerals, making them unavailable to the body. While this might be useful in the case of iron, preventing it producing harmful free radicals through oxidation, it is unhelpful when phytates bind up antioxidant nutrients such as copper and zinc.

Plant hormones (phytoestrogens)

These are chemically similar to human oestrogens which are thought to reduce the risk of breast cancer.

Plant phenols and indoles

These are responsible for some nasty smells (such as when cabbage is cut and when vegetables rot). In laboratory and animal experiments these substances have stopped or slowed down the activity of free radical-like cancer-causing chemicals. In animal studies, they appear to reduce the incidence of chemically-induced cancers of the breast, lung and stomach.

Retinol (vitamin A) and riboflavin (vitamin B2)

These have been called preventive antioxidant vitamins because they have a general role in keeping cells healthy rather than directly preventing oxidation or trapping free radicals.

Uric acid

Uric acid is a by-product of digesting protein and a troublesome substance if you are prone to gout or kidney stones. However, it might act as an antioxidant outside cells, though this is not yet proven.

Can antioxidants in alcohol protect you?

While you don't have to drink to be healthy, moderate drinkers (those who drink 1½–2 units a day) suffer less heart disease, diabetes, gallstones, some cancers and other illnesses than non-drinkers or those who drink only very occasionally. Scientific studies have consistently come up with a U-shaped curve putting teetotallers and heavy drinkers at the top of each upright of the U (where they have the greatest risk) and moderate drinkers at the base of the U.

Whether the antioxidants in some alcoholic drinks are giving a protective effect remains to be proved on a large scale. Any benefits could be due to a combination of ingredients. However, there are non-alcoholic substances (phenols) in red wine that have antioxidant powers to stop oxidative damage to cholesterol and so reduce heart disease.

It seems that alcohol itself may protect against heart disease in several ways:

- It raises levels of the good type of cholesterol (HDL).
- It lowers platelet aggregation (part of the process in which cholesterol builds up in the arteries).
- It lowers the level of fibrinogen (a substance necessary to blood clotting).

Some experts go so far as to say that no disease can be associated with one or two drinks a day – and that drinking at that level doesn't kill off your brain cells. Moderate drinkers also have fewer colds than teetotallers and heavy drinkers.

Even so, alcohol is still a toxin that the body has to detoxify, a process that can leave you deficient in the ACE nutrient vitamin C, B vitamins and some minerals. Unfortunately alcohol (like sugar) doesn't come complete with the vitamins and minerals needed to digest the calories – and because it is a diuretic (i.e. it stimulates urination) it makes you lose more vitamin C. So unless your diet is rich in ACE nutrient foods you won't benefit from moderate drinking and you could be left short of the vitamins needed to stop you catching a cold and to keep up your immunity to other illnesses.

Can polyunsaturates be harmful?

Many people have switched to polyunsaturated vegetable oils for health reasons, the aim being to reduce saturated fat intake and minimize the risk of heart disease. However, there has been concern that overheating polyunsaturated oils, which are much less stable when heated than monounsaturated oils such as olive oil and rapeseed oil, and saturated fats like lard and butter, might lead to the creation of harmful free radicals during cooking.

There is also controversy over whether cooking at high temperatures with polyunsaturated fats might increase the production of trans fats (see page 81). This is being investigated because trans fats, like saturated fats, raise blood cholesterol levels, increasing the risk of coronary heart disease.

However, as long as you don't use your cooking oil more than eight times and don't heat it to a temperature higher than 170°C/335°F (to the point where it produces blue smoke) there would seem to be no risk of free-radical damage.

When is an antioxidant not an antioxidant?

While vitamin C and beta carotene act as protective antioxidants 99 per cent of the time, they are what is known as 'redox' agents. This means they can be both antioxidant and pro-oxidant – in other words, they can be harmful 1 per cent of the time! In their pro-oxidant role they encourage oxidation and the production of free radicals. The same is true of the mineral copper.

If taken in mega-doses vitamin C can, if there's a lot of iron around in the body, bring about higher levels of the type of iron that might promote cancer. Vitamin C also helps the body absorb vegetarian sources of iron, and too much iron might also increase the risk of heart disease as well as aggravating arthritis.

CHAPTER 3

What Happens If You Don't Eat Up Your Greens?

Since discovering that people who eat too little fruit and vegetables (and therefore have a low intake of ACE nutrients) are at greater risk of cancer, heart disease and other ills than those who eat a good amount, scientists have used dietary supplements (vitamin and mineral pills) in trials designed to try to prevent, or cure, illness. To investigate the role of ACE nutrients, scientists have several options:

1. They can feed animals on diets high or low in ACE foods, measure the incidence of cancer and do some complicated guesswork to translate the likelihood of the same thing happening in humans.
2. They can give people who already have a disease a different diet or supplements of, for example, vitamins and minerals, fish oil or evening primrose oil to see if an improvement results. In some trials not everyone receives the treatment so that its effect can be better judged by comparing the state of health of the recipients with that of the people who aren't treated.
3. They can identify populations where not many people get the disease under investigation and see if they develop the disease when they move to other cultures and adopt different diets and lifestyles.
4. They can study trends such as the increasing rates of heart disease and cancer in the Western world and then look back at changes in diet and lifestyle to see if there is any correlation.

5. They can ask people who have a disease what their diet and lifestyle was in the past and compare it with that of people of the same age and sex who don't have the disease.

6 They can do 'prospective' studies in which they take samples (blood, urine, DNA) from healthy people and then wait for them to get a disease to see how their nutritional status, diet, genes and so on differ from those who don't get it.

What follows is a look at some of the scientific evidence that highlights the importance of ACE nutrients – or, to put it another way, here's fair warning of some of the things that might happen to you if you don't eat up your greens!

Heart disease

First, let's recap on the general picture:

1. Dietary surveys in various countries have shown that the greater the amount of fruit and vegetables eaten (and hence the greater the intake of ACE nutrients), the less heart disease occurs.

2. In European countries, men with heart disease have been shown to have lower intakes of vitamins E and C although the evidence is not so strong for beta carotene and selenium.

Now let's look at some more specific examples:

● Large doses of vitamin E supplements gave protection against heart disease in two American studies of nearly 133,000 people conducted by Harvard Medical School. More than 87,000 female nurses aged 34–59 who took more than 149mg per day of vitamin E a day for two years had only half the number of heart attacks as women of similar age and circumstances who did not take the vitamin and more than 45,500 men aged 40–75 who took it for more than two years had a 26 per cent lower risk than their fellow health workers. The protective power of vitamin E was stronger than for vitamin C or beta carotene. Mega-doses (above 596mg daily) gave no extra benefit. The supplements taken were in both natural (from soy and other vegetable oils) and synthetic forms. The protective effect was not seen in people whose only source of vitamin E was their diet.

- In the Harvard Physicians Study, 22,000 male doctors are being studied as part of a ten-year project. This is the study that established the benefits of aspirin in the prevention of heart disease. The beta-carotene part of the study should be completed in 1996. So far it has been noticed that 333 men who began the study with signs of heart disease (but not heart attacks) and who were taking 50mg beta carotene a day had only half as many 'vascular events' (heart attack, stroke, bypasses, sudden cardiac deaths) as their fellow health workers. But this is only preliminary information and there might be a dual effect of aspirin preventing blood clotting and beta carotene preventing the oxidization of cholesterol by free radicals which allows arteries to become clogged up, increasing the risk of heart disease. Now the researchers are looking at 45,000 post-menopausal women to see if a similar effect occurs.

- In the MONICA (Monitoring of Cardiovascular Disease) study a random selection of middle-aged men in 16 European populations from Finland to Spain have been studied for their heart disease risks. High blood cholesterol and blood pressure were strong risk factors and the men who had them also had low levels of vitamin E. Associations with low vitamin C levels only showed up when cholesterol was above 5.7 mmol/litre on average. (The desirable level for individuals is not above 5.2 mmol/litre.) Vitamin C helps vitamin E regenerate its antioxidant powers which protect against heart disease.

- In a study of Scottish men, those who had angina had far lower ACE nutrient levels than those who had no evidence of heart disease. Vitamin E seemed to be the key ACE nutrient in this respect.

- A study comparing the thickness of the carotid artery among Finnish men over a two-year period showed that those who had the greatest thickening had the lowest levels of vitamin C and selenium.

Cancer

The world's largest survey of links between diet and cancer started in Europe in 1992, with half a million people supplying details of diet and giving blood and urine samples which will be kept under special conditions (to preserve vitamin content in particular) for up to 20 years. This EPIC (European Prospective Investigation of Cancer) study will allow researchers to compare the ACE intake, and status, of people who go on to develop cancer with those of their peers who remain disease-free.

This will solve one of researchers' biggest problems of testing theories about oxidative (free radical) stress and the damage it does to health. Obviously it is not ethical to expose people to free radicals to see if they develop cancer, so prospective studies such as EPIC are done to allow diet and antioxidant status to be measured for years before cancer develops.

In addition, other major clinical trials of ACE nutrients and cancer are now in progress and one has just finished:

- In the Linxian province of China, where there are some of the highest rates of stomach and oesophageal cancer in the world, a five-year study among 30,000 Chinese who were given antioxidant vitamin supplements resulted in a 13 per cent drop in the expected number of deaths from cancer, especially stomach cancer. Various combinations of vitamins and minerals were taken: one group took beta carotene, vitamin E and selenium; one vitamin A and zinc; one riboflavin and niacin; and one vitamin C and molybdenum. The best resuts were from the group taking 15mg of beta carotene, 30mg of vitamin E amd 50mcg selenium daily. While the study supports the view that ACE nutrients can help ward off disease, it's important to remember that many rural Chinese such as those in the study have a very restricted diet, low in vitamins and minerals.

- In Finland, 29,000 smokers are participating in a trial in which beta carotene and vitamin E are being given together to see whether this combination of nutrients can help prevent lung cancer in these high risk individuals.

- In the US, the CARET (Carotene and Retinol Efficacy Trial) is testing the effects of beta carotene and retinol (vitamin A) on former heavy smokers and asbestos-exposed workers who have smoked and who are therefore at high risk of cancer. It is hoped that 18,000 men and women will be recruited for the trial, due to finish in 1998.

Other health factors that might be affected by ACE nutrients

Ageing – slowing down the process

ACE nutrients can't reverse the ageing process – whatever anyone tells you to the contrary – but they can probably help you look younger and stay healthier for longer because they help to prevent free-radical damage to many organs, including damage that leads to wrinkles, caused by exposure to too much sun.

Two common problems among the over-60s are cataracts (see page 42) and poor immunity – older people often say that it takes them longer to get over infections. In one Canadian trial, 100 people over the age of 65 were given a multi-vitamin and multi-mineral tablet with extra vitamin E and beta carotene; others received a placebo (dummy) tablet. The group that took the supplement had half as many incidences of colds, flu and other infections as the other group (meaning also that they needed less treatment with antibiotics) and when they did fall ill they recovered in half the time. Other similar small studies in the US have shown better immunity among healthy older people taking 1192mg of vitamin E a day. In both cases the supplemented people were also given a diet well-balanced in other nutrients. The reason vitamin E is thought to help boost immunity is that it turns off production of a substance called prostaglandin E2, which increases with age and depresses the immune system.

Alzheimer's disease

Patients with Alzheimer's disease have higher than normal levels of two enzymes involved in fighting free radicals. In studies, they have also been shown to have lower levels of vitamin E, beta carotene and vitamin A compared with people of the same age (74–90) not affected by the disease and eating a diet containing the same amount of nutrients. If an increase in damage to nerve cells from free radicals is involved in the disease, ACE nutrients such as vitamin E and beta carotene may slow its progress. Since vitamins A and E and carotenes are free-radical scavengers, a diet that leaves you short of them could worsen dementia.

Arthritis

As anyone who has had arthritis knows, it involves pain, swelling and stiffness in the joint(s). There are several types of arthritis but the most common ones, rheumatoid arthritis and osteoarthritis, involve inflammation of the joint(s). Inflammatory cells produce free radicals, and the continual production in an arthritic joint probably exhausts the supply of ACE nutrients so that the antioxidant control process fails. Evidence that a diet rich in vitamins A, E and the mineral selenium protects against arthritis comes from Finland where people with low levels of these nutrients have been shown to go on to get rheumatoid arthritis. Interestingly, iron deficiency may also protect against arthritis, as the presence of iron can lead to oxidation.

Asthma and breathing problems

Asthma has doubled in the last 20 years among young children which some scientists attribute to the drop in consumption of fresh fruit and vegetables (for ACE vitamins) and fresh fish and meat (for ACE minerals) rather than environmental pollution. The reason? The inflammatory process in asthma generates free radicals and increases susceptibility to asthma-causing allergens. And the lungs probably depend on eating enough ACE nutrients for their defence.

People who hardly ever eat fresh fruit and vegetables risk impaired lung function on a par with smokers. In one study those who never drank fresh fruit juice and who ate fresh fruit less than once a week breathed out less efficiently (a measure of lung function) regardless of whether or not they smoked. Those who ate fruit daily had the best lung measurements. This might explain why not all smokers suffer from emphysema and bronchitis and other breathing problems

Cataracts

The older you are the more likely you are to develop cataracts and macular (the centre of the retina) degeneration (the commonest cause of blindness in the UK, accounting for one-third of sight impairment in the over-55s).

No one knows exactly what causes cataracts, but a popular

theory is that ultra-violet rays oxidize protein in the lens, spoiling its crystal-clear structure and blurring vision. Antioxidant vitamins might give some protection to the retina. Vitamin C in particular is found in high concentrations in the eye, where it may be acting as an antioxidant to counteract the production of oxygen free radicals produced by the effect of light on the eye.

In one study of more than 50,000 American women aged 45 and over, those who took vitamin C and beta carotene in the long term had lower risk of cataracts severe enough to need an operation. The study found that those who had the highest food intake of vitamin A and beta carotene had a 39 per cent lower risk of cataracts than women with the lowest intake. However, this was not as good as the women who used vitamin C supplements for ten or more years. Spinach was the food most consistently associated with lower relative risk rather than carrots, which have previously been thought of as the vegetable for eye health.

In addition, a clinical trial to test whether vitamins C, E and beta carotene protect against cataract development is in progress at the Nuffield Laboratories in Oxford. The study will see whether ACE vitamin supplements can slow down cataract development once it has started.

Some studies suggest that people with macular degeneration eat less carotene-rich fruits and vegetables than those without eye problems, but no less vitamin C. Some have lower levels of vitamin E. An American study of people who had suffered macular degeneration in one eye suggests that eating a diet rich in ACE nutrients might slow down the process in the other eye.

Excessive exposure of the eye to ultra-violet radiation can damage the retina, irritate the cornea (leading to snow blindness) and contribute to clouding of the lens (as in cataracts). Dangers can be reduced by wearing sunglasses that are effective at blocking out the harmful UV rays (i.e. sunglasses that conform to British Standard (BS) 2724).

Cervical cancer

It's known that women are more at risk of this disease if they commence sexual activity at a young age, if they have a history of sexually transmitted diseases, if they smoke or if they have genital warts, particularly of the cervix. However, all these risk factors are uncommon among Native American women, who have a high incidence of cervical cancer. On the evidence of surveys comparing the diet of Native American women with similar women without the disease, it has been suggested that low intakes of ACE nutrients might account for the high rate of cervical cancer and pre-cancerous conditions among these women. The affected women all showed low intakes of vitamins C, E and folic acid. The theory is plausible, as low intakes of these nutrients have been associated with increased risk in other populations.

Colorectal cancers

The possible benefits of antioxidants to people with pre-cancerous conditions of the colon and rectum are beginning to be investigated. Studies on animals show that vitamins A, C and E may all be protective. However, it is difficult to study the effect of vitamins because these cancers take many years to develop. In one study researchers examined the effect of six months of treatment with a combination of vitamins A, C and E on proliferation of cells (an indicator of increased cancer risk) in the rectal mucosa of patients who had been treated for adenomas (pre-cancerous polyps). Compared with patients who received placebos, the vitamin-supplemented patients had fewer cell abnormalities.

Other studies of colorectal cancer in Finland, the US, Switzerland and Britain have compared the level of vitamin E in the blood of healthy people taken 14 years previously with vitamin E levels in those who have gone on to develop colonic or rectal cancers. Detailed analysis revealed that the quarter of those tested with the highest vitamin E levels did have a slightly lower cancer risk.

In general, a diet that includes lots of fruit, vegetables and starchy food (and is therefore high in fibre and ACE nutrients) and is low in fat and meat gives the lowest risk of colorectal cancer. Meat may be a particular problem because the substances called amines that form in cooked meat (especially meat that has been grilled or fried) may produce mutations in DNA in the large gut, predisposing to cancer.

Cystic fibrosis

Many children with cystic fibrosis have an impaired ability to absorb antioxidants (and other nutrients). Their diets are usually supplemented with additional vitamins and minerals. Studies are now going on to see if a lack of ACE nutrients contributes to their reduced ability to withstand oxidative damage and may also be associated with their breathing problems and susceptibility to cancer.

Exercise

Taking exercise increases the need for ACE nutrients because the extra oxygen burned raises free-radical levels in muscles and the liver by two to three times. Animal studies suggest that vitamin E supplementation reduces the free-radical production. Many top athletes do take vitamin supplements to speed recovery after strenuous exercise.

Human sperm

The quality of human sperm has been deteriorating for 50 years. As damage to genetic material can lead to birth defects, genetic diseases and cancer it's important to find out why and correct the situation. Studies in America indicate that damaged sperm DNA in healthy men is more common if there are low levels of vitamin C in the diet. For example, men eating 250mg of vitamin C a day had normal sperm, but when the vitamin C content was reduced to a very low 5mg double the number of damaged DNA appeared. Increasing the vitamin C to 20mg a day did not help much and the level of damaged (oxidized) DNA continued to reach 250 per cent more than initial levels. Bringing the diet back up to 250mg a day reduced levels of damaged DNA by 36 per cent. While all sperm will never be 'perfect', researchers conclude that 200–250mg of vitamin C a day produces the best quality sperm.

Mental health

Women who eat more fruit and vegetables report better mental health, according to a small-scale study by one psychologist. In the same study of 1000 people, chosen at random for a postal survey, there was no association in men between mood and the amount of fruit and vegetables consumed. One explanation offered by researchers is that mood improvement may be linked to the higher vitamin and mineral intake associated with the fresh food diet. Or it might just be that happy women eat more vegetables!

Mouth conditions

A major American study has found a strong association between the use of vitamin E supplements and reduced risk of mouth cancer. Taking into account smoking and drinking alcohol, it was found that people who took supplements of vitamins A, B complex, C or E had a lower risk of oral cancer than those who did not. Vitamin E showed the most significant protective effect. Those who had ever used vitamin E regularly for six months or more halved their risk.

Cancer of the oesophagus is associated with drinking alcohol and smoking. The risk is 15 times greater if you do both. However, in countries where a lot of fruit and vegetables are eaten there are fewer deaths from oesophageal cancers, regardless of smoking and drinking habits. *Warning:* if you are a smoker do not interpret that finding to mean that eating lots of fruit and vegetables will protect you against cancer (or other smoker's diseases such as bronchitis and general respiratory problems).

Several small trials are also underway using beta carotene, which is essentially non-toxic and without side-effects, to see if pre-cancerous conditions of the mouth (currently treated with vitamin A and related compounds which cause side-effects) can do any better. So far about half the patients have had a good response.

Premature babies

Premature babies have lower than normal levels of vitamin E in their blood, and they remain deficient in it for up to two months because their immature digestive systems can't absorb it. This may be one reason why some develop chronic lung disease. British research is currently trying to find out more about the protective role of vitamin E for these babies.

Skin and the thinning ozone layer

Ozone is a form of oxygen covering the planet with a 32km/20 mile-thick blanket that absorbs most of the sun's ultra-violet (UV) rays. Without the ozone layer, life on earth would be scorched to a frazzle. Holes and thinning in the ozone layer (caused by man-made pollution) mean more UV radiation is reaching earth, increasing the risk of skin cancer and causing premature ageing of the skin. It's well known that sunbathing and exposure to sun-light accelerate ageing in skin by oxidative damage. Experiments in the laboratory show that ozone reacts with polyunsaturated fat in cells to form free radicals, leading to wrinkles and skin blemishes. In fact, it's well known that exposure to sunlight accel-erates ageing in skin. ACE nutrients are also damaged or destroyed in the skin when it is exposed to UV radiation. Researchers are trying to establish if exposure to sunlight increases the need for antioxidant nutrients in the skin. So far animal experiments show that vitamin E supplementation reduces skin damage.

But I don't like cabbage...

Eating up your greens can be difficult if you carry the gene that makes you sensitive to the PTC (phenylthiocarbamide) crystals in the cabbage family because it makes vegetables like brussels sprouts and broccoli unacceptably bitter. One theory is that PTC sensitivity evolved because brassicas contain high levels of goitro-gens – substances that bind with iodine and may, in certain cir-cumstances, lead to goitres. Once upon a time this might have been important, but today we have different strains of brassicas and a lot of other influences on our choice of foods. So when chil-dren refuse to eat up their greens, it is up to you whether you give them the benefit of the PTC doubt, or decide that they are being faddy eaters!

CHAPTER 4

Take the ACE Pledge

Given the choice, the way I would increase my intake of ACE nutrients is to move to the Mediterranean and adopt the lifestyle (including the diet) that characterizes that sunny part of the world. But, for those of us who live in Britain, the best alternative is to follow *The Ultimate ACE Diet* – and fortunately, the wide range of foods now available makes this easy to do.

ACE Mediterranean clues

Large groups of people living in the Mediterranean eat a lot of fat in the form of oil – and although, as you have noticed on holidays, some do grow fat, they do not suffer the same amount of coronary heart disease as exists in Britain. While the French have weight problems from a diet rich in both oil and animal fat in charcuterie and cheese, they have the lowest heart disease of any industrialized nation except Japan.

Why? Are they genetically different? That is to say, do they have a built-in protective mechanism that allows them to eat lots of fat and get away with it? As far as we know, they do not. By looking in more detail at what they eat, scientists have concluded that different dietary patterns throughout Europe explain the differing rates of heart disease and cancer.

The ones who stay healthy are the ones who eat large quantities of fruit and vegetables, regardless of whether they eat a lot or a little starchy food or a lot or a little fat (although, on the whole, the ones who are healthy eat only small amounts of *saturated* fat). The amount of fruit eaten by the British each year is much lower than in other European countries.

Table 11: Fruit consumption in kilograms eaten per person per year	
Italy	80
Greece	70
Spain	62
Netherlands	61
Germany	60
France	60
Britain	40

Table 12: Vegetable consumption (excluding potatoes) in kilograms eaten per person per year	
Greece	215
Spain	210
Italy	150
France	130
Netherlands	100
Germany	56
Britain	53

The amount of fat eaten by the British is also higher than that eaten in traditional Mediterranean countries.

Table 13: Butter and margarine consumption in kilograms eaten per person per year	
Netherlands	12.5
Germany	12.5
Britain	12
France	12
Greece	4
Spain	3
Italy	3

Figures from EPIC (European Prospective Investigation of Cancer).

Fruit and vegetable pledge

Try to eat at least five portions of fruit and vegetables a day, which amounts to around 400g/14oz. Include 30g/1oz of pulses, seeds and nuts, especially if you are vegetarian. But don't limit yourself to this amount of fruit and vegetables – the more you eat the better.

This will probably mean changing the way you plan your meals because it places less importance on meat, fish or cheese and more on including several portions of vegetables with a main course and eating fruit for dessert. It also means including a lot of

Table 14: A typical day's eating		
	Before The Ultimate ACE Diet	*With The Ultimate ACE Diet*
Breakfast	Sugary breakfast cereal, white toast, spread and preserves	Fruit juice and/or fresh fruit or prunes chopped onto high-fibre, low-sugar breakfast cereal, or half grapefruit, wholemeal toast with spread rich in vitamin E
Mid-morning	Biscuits or confectionery	Piece of fresh fruit
Lunch	Cheese or meat and pickle sand-wich. Slice of cake or chocolate bar	Low-fat cheese (or less cheese) or lean meat sandwich with lots of salad. Piece of fruit or fruit yogurt
Main meal	Meat, potatoes and 1 portion of veg, or spaghetti and meatballs	Lean meat or fish, potatoes (in skin), 2 portions of veg, or spaghetti and meatballs with salad
Pudding	2–3 scoops ice-cream	1 scoop ice-cream and fresh fruit
Snacks	Confectionery, chocolate, biscuits, cakes	Fresh fruit, low-fat fruit yogurt, fruit cake, currant bun, *occasional* chocolate bar

starchy foods such as bread, pasta, rice and potatoes, and finally, making meat, fish and cheese or other dairy produce a smaller component of the meal.

Fruit

Each of the fruits listed below equals 1 portion, unless stated otherwise:

Apple
Avocado pear, ½
Apricots, fresh or semi-dried, 4
Banana
Blackberries, raspberries, blackcurrants, cherries, gooseberries, stewed rhubarb and other cooked fruit, around 100g/3½oz
Clementine or other citrus such as mandarin, mineola, orange, tangerine, satsuma
Damsons, greengages or other small plums, 4
Dates, fresh or dried, 4–6
Figs, fresh or dried 4
Grapefruit, ½
Grapes, 100g/3½oz
Kiwifruit, 2
Mango, ½
Melon, 175g/6oz
Nectarine
Passion fruit, 4–5
Papaw, ½
Peach
Pear
Pineapple, 75–100g/3–3½oz
Prunes, stewed 6, semi-dried 4
Sharon fruit (persimmon)
Watermelon, 200g/7oz

Fruit juice

1 citrus fruit, squeezed
200ml/7fl oz glass
Individual carton

Table 15: Britain's favourite fresh fruits	Britain's favourite fresh vegetables
1. Bananas	1. Potatoes
2. Apples (dessert)	2. Tomatoes*
3. Strawberries*	3. Lettuce
4. Oranges*	4. Carrots*
5. Peaches*	5. Onions
6. Pears	6. Cauliflower*
7. Grapes	7. Cabbage*
8. Satsumas/clementines/ tangerines*	8. Mushrooms
	9. Spring onions
9. Cherries	10. Brussels sprouts*
10. Melon (Cantaloupe*)	
* Good source of ACE nutrients	* Good source of ACE nutrients

Vegetables

Portions are around 75–100g/3–3½oz. This is shown below in terms of large (15ml) tablespoonfuls. You can eat more, of course; the list is just a rough guide to give you an idea of the variety of vegetables available.

Artichoke, globe
Asparagus spears, 5
Baked beans
Broad beans, 2 tbsp
French and runner beans
Bean sprouts, 8 tbsp
Broccoli and calabrese spears, 2 medium-large ones
Brussels sprouts, 9–10
Cabbage
Carrots, 2 tbsp
Cauliflower, 8 florets
Celery, 3 sticks

Chickpeas, 2–3 tbsp, cooked
Chinese leaf, 2 large leaves
Coleslaw, low fat, 2 tbsp
Corn on the cob, 1 ear
Cucumber, 5cm/2 inch slice
Green banana, ½
Leek
Lentils, 2½–3 tbsp, cooked
Lettuce, 16 leaves
Marrow
Mushrooms, poached, 10
Mustard and cress, ½ punnet equals ¼ portion
Okra, 8 equals ¼ portion
Onion, 1½–2
Parsnips, 1 medium
Peas, 3 tbsp
Pepper
Plantain ⅓–½
Ratatouille, 3 tbsp
Sauerkraut, 3 tbsp
Spinach
Swede
Sweetcorn (corn on the cob)
Tomatoes, 1 large or 6 cherry
Turnip
Watercress, 1 bunch

How to eat more fruit

Breakfast

Breakfast is one of the most convenient times to add more fruit to
your diet.

- Top your favourite breakfast cereal with a sliced banana or 3–4
  stewed or no-need-to-soak prunes.
- Grate an apple and stir it into your muesli. In Germany and
  Austria, where muesli originated, some people soak the muesli
  overnight in milk or apple juice then stir in seasonal fresh fruit

at the breakfast table. Others assemble their own blend of muesli by mixing together at the breakfast table a bowlful of goodies from containers of oats, flaked rice and other grains, linseed or other seeds such as pumpkin or sunflower; dried fruit (raisins, apricots, prunes, figs, peaches) and nuts such as hazelnuts, almonds, brazils or cashews.

- Soft fruit such as strawberries and raspberries go well with cereals and muesli.
- Stir some sultanas or chopped dried apricots into bran flakes.
- Stir some raisins or sultanas into porridge.
- Serve a half grapefruit with some prunes.
- Drink freshly squeezed orange juice.
- Top fresh fruit salad with yogurt, or enjoy it on its own.
- Make a dried fruit compote of prunes, apricots, raisins or dried apple.
- For an exotic treat, serve a Caribbean breakfast of sliced papaw (papaya), pineapple, banana and grapefruit.
- For an exotic Indian breakfast serve sliced mango with lassi or the equivalent Western drinking yogurt.

Main courses

- Recipes from around the world make much of the combination of meat and fruit. The French use both dried and fresh fruit. Apples, prunes, apricots, quince and currants have been used with meat since medieval times in the Arab world, and since Tudor days in Britain. The Scandinavians are fond of serving berries (rich in ACE nutrients) with meat and even fish dishes. You will find many more examples in cookery books and on menus.

Puddings

- You don't need me to tell you how to make a fruit salad, as you have probably often chopped or diced fruit in your own favourite combinations. However, try to make the most of ACE fruit such as citrus fruits, strawberries, raspberries, blackcurrants, apricots, mango and melon. Add the prepared fruit to a fruit juice base such as apple or orange juice rather than a sugar syrup. Experiment with colour themes, for example by using fruits all of one colour or by making attractive combinations such as green and yellow or orange. Alternatively, serve fruit in simpler combinations such as halved papaw (papaya) dressed with fresh lime juice and filled with fresh strawberries.

- Fruit kebabs are a novel idea and are especially suitable as canapés for drinks parties and buffets, while children will find fruit on a stick more fun than just plain fruit. Jellies made from real fruit and real fruit juice are also loved by all ages (see Chapter 7).

- Traditional British fruits such as gooseberries, blackcurrants, rhubarb and apples can be cooked and cooled before being mixed with Greek yogurt or low-fat natural yogurt to make fruit fools. Dried fruits such as prunes and apricots are equally good. Uncooked but puréed soft fruits such as strawberries and raspberries are also suitable, as is mango. Sweeten to taste, if need be, although many fruits are sweet enough.

- Peaches, pineapples and bananas are especially good on the barbecue or under the grill. Baste the cut fruit during cooking with lemon or lime juice mixed with honey, or wrap the fruit halves or slices in greaseproof paper and foil and cook in the embers. Banana skins go black but the fruit inside is not discoloured.

Snacks

- Fresh fruit is one of the most convenient snack foods. A piece of fruit will add far more ACE nutrients to your life than a biscuit, chocolate bar, crisps or other confectionery.

- Dried fruit, especially in the handy little snack packs, is easy to carry in a child's lunchbox, a school bag or a handbag.

- Nuts are rich in vitamin E – but salted nuts can add too much sodium to the diet, so opt for unsalted. Nuts are also preferred to sweets by dentists because they don't cause caries (holes) in your teeth – and, unlike many snacks, they are high in fibre. Surveys also show that vegetarians who eat a lot of nuts (as part of a low-fat diet) are less likely to suffer coronary heart disease, possibly because of their vitamin E or monounsaturated fat content. However, while nuts are highly nutritious they are also high in calories, so don't go mad and eat huge amounts as snacks. (And be careful about giving them to small children, who might choke on them.)

- Seeds such as sunflower and pumpkin (and pine kernels) share the benefits – and high calories – of nuts.
- Trail mix – home-made or bought mixtures of raisins, seeds, banana chips, coconut flakes, dried apricots etc. – is useful when you're feeling peckish.

Shopping, storing and preparing fruit and vegetables

Food shopping can be a chore, but it becomes a delight when considering the colourful array of fruit and vegetables in street markets and on supermarket shelves. Make the most of seasonal fruit and vegetables as they are often the cheapest – and, if locally produced, they may also be the freshest.

When shopping for fruit and vegetables it's important to select for quality and freshness and to know how long the produce will last without deteriorating, so you don't buy it too early. When you have got your produce home, store it so as to retain its freshness and prepare it properly to retain maximum vitamin and mineral content.

An A-Z of Everyday and ACE fruit

= ACE fruit rich in ACE nutrients

General guidelines

- Prepare as near to cooking or serving as possible. Try to avoid preparing in advance and leaving in water or uncovered in the fridge.
- Wash and scrub fruit and vegetables to remove surface pesticides and bacteria. Add a few drops of soap or washing up liquid to help shift unwanted substances. Rinse well in cold water.
- Always serve immediately after cooking.
- Once cut, dress cut surfaces with lemon or lime juice, cover and store in the fridge.

- Always keep out of direct sunlight, even if storing at room temperature.
- Eat raw fruit and vegetables as often as possible, because even quick cooking reduces the vitamin and mineral content of fruit and vegetables.
- Avoid unnecessary peeling, as much of the vitamin and mineral content is just below the skin. Peeling also wastes valuable fibre.
- Avoid unnecessary chopping as it provides more surface area from which vitamins and minerals can leach into water.

Apples

- Autumn is when the new fruit is ready, but apples are stored in controlled atmospheric conditions that delay their ripening so that they are available all year round. Choose firm, bright crisp apples.
- Don't buy fruit with damaged or wrinkled, tired-looking skin.
- Store in the fridge for a couple of weeks to retain the crispness, but bring to room temperature before eating.
- Wash well. Use soapy water if you want to remove the protective wax used on most apples and rinse it off well. Organic apples will not have been coated with wax. There is no need to peel. If cutting apples up, toss in lemon juice to prevent browning and prepare as near to cooking/serving as possible.

* Apricots

- Buy in May–July, when they should be firm and plump with bright, downy skin.
- Don't buy unripe fruit as it's often disappointing and dry and avoid old, wrinkled apricots.
- Store in the fridge for up to a week, or ripen in a brown paper bag at room temperature.
- Wash and eat raw or poach lightly.

Avocados

- Buy all year round. Choose even-coloured avocados with unblemished skin. Never trust the 'ripe' or 'ready to eat' labels; such fruit is often overripe and soft. The fruit should still be quite firm.

- Don't buy fruit with bruises or brown scarring on the skin as this often indicates stringy brown and bruised flesh.
- Store at room temperature for up to a week, depending how ripe the fruit is. If it's already ripe, keep it in the fridge and use within a couple of days.
- To prepare, halve the fruit, running a knife around the circumference through the flesh to the central stone. Twist the halves apart and remove the stone. To remove the skin slip the end of a teaspoon between flesh and skin to loosen, then lift off. Dress in lemon juice or vinaigrette to prevent browning.

Bananas
- Buy all year round, choosing yellow fruit with a small number of brown specks if you want it for immediate use, or fruit with green ends if it is to have time to ripen.
- Don't buy soft, overripe fruit with very brown skins.
- Store at room temperature for a week, although the fruit will progressively ripen during this time. Don't be tempted to put it in the fridge as this turns the skin black and unattractive.
- To prepare, you can simply peel and eat! If you are going to cook bananas, toss in lemon juice to prevent discoloration.

* Blackberries
- Buy in late summer and autumn. A uniform black colour indicates ripeness, as does a 'bloom', especially on hedgerow fruit.
- Don't buy if showing signs of mould or if damaged so that the juice has run out of the fruit.
- Store in the fridge, unwashed and uncovered, until ready for use. Blackberries go mouldy quickly, so use as soon as possible.
- To prepare, wash and dry gently on absorbent kitchen paper or a clean teatowel (an old one that you don't mind being stained from the juice).

* Currants (black, red, white)
- Buy in summer when the fruit is firm, whole, plump and shiny.
- Don't buy if showing signs of mould or if damaged so that the juice has run out of the fruit.
- Store in the fridge, unwashed and uncovered, for a couple of days.

- To prepare, top and tail. Some people find it easier if the fruit is frozen first on its sprigs so the hardened berries can be pulled off; this causes less damage to the fruit. Rinse and pat dry on absorbent kitchen paper or a clean teatowel.

* Grapefruit

- Buy all year. Choose firm, well-shaped, round fruit.
- Don't buy misshapen fruit with bruises or other soft patches on the skin.
- Store in the fridge or at room temperature. As with oranges, the thick skin keeps in the moisture and most citrus fruit is also waxed (sometimes with a fungicide) to retain moisture and prevent mould.
- To prepare, halve and remove the seeds. Loosen the segments with a serrated knife if serving as breakfast halves. Alternatively, remove the peel and cut into segments for other uses.

Grapes

- Buy all year round. Choose well-shaped grapes that are plump with tight skins. They may be shiny or have a soft bloom.
- Don't buy if the grapes are shrivelled and wrinkled, if they show signs of going brown, or if they are split, wet and sticky.
- Store in the fridge for four or five days.
- To prepare, wash when ready to eat and pat dry on absorbent kitchen paper or a clean teatowel.

* Kiwifruit

- Buy all year round, though they are most readily available and cheapest in winter. The brown hairy skin should be covering firm fruit that yields only slightly when pressed.
- Don't buy if damaged or soft.
- Store at room temperature or in the fridge. As the fruit continues to ripen storage time will depend on how ripe they were when bought, but they should keep for up to two weeks without going soft.
- To prepare, peel and slice for use in recipes, or halve and eat with a teaspoon. The black seeds are edible.

* Lemons and limes

- Buy fruit with hard, gleaming rind and undamaged skin. Choose lemons that feel heavy for their weight and don't have very thick skin. If you want to use the skin (zest) choose unwaxed or organic fruit.
- Don't buy if soft, shrivelled or browning.
- Store at room temperature or in the fridge. Lemons and limes won't ripen further.
- Use the flesh, zest or juice as required. Remove pips before putting slices in drinks or serving wedges for squeezing over food.

* Mangoes

- Buy all year round. Choose smooth, firm-skinned fruit that is not too soft when pressed. Skin colour depends on variety.
- Don't buy if the skin is wrinkled or blemished with spots and black specks.
- Store in the fridge for about three days if ripe or at room temperature if the fruit needs to ripen.
- To prepare, peel and slice from the large flat central stone.

* Melons

- Buy in late summer for the best bargains, though they are available all year. All the varieties should have a reasonably unblemished, even-coloured skin. Some are more scented than others and some scent at the stalk end is an indication of ripeness. The colour of the flesh depends upon variety, but all should be evenly coloured; a line of darker flesh near the skin indicates that the fruit is unripe.
- Don't buy if damaged or bruised. It is best to buy whole melons as these keep better than ready-cut wedges.
- Store either in the fridge or at room temperature for up to two weeks – it does not matter which as melons do not continue to ripen after picking. Once cut, wrap and store in the fridge.
- Prepare by cutting into wedges or in half, removing the seeds.

* Oranges

- Buy different varieties all year round. Whatever the variety, a fruit that seems heavy for its size with an thin, even, undamaged skin is best. If you want to use the zest choose unwaxed or organic fruit.

- Don't buy wrinkled, dry-looking fruit with soft or bruised areas on the skin.
- Store at room temperature for about ten days, or in the fridge if you need to keep them longer.
- Use the zest, flesh or juice as required. Remove the pips before putting slices in drinks and salads.

* Pawpaws (papayas)

- Buy all year, choosing firm fruit that has a bright and even-coloured skin. If it feels slightly soft it is ripe.
- Don't buy fruit with brown marks on the skin, soft spots or bruises. Avoid wrinkled old-looking fruit, and any that is very soft.
- Store at room temperature for a couple of days, or, if ripe, in the fridge.
- Pawpaws are usually halved, when the black seeds can be removed easily with a spoon. Dress with lime juice before serving.

* Peaches and nectarines

- Buy in summer. The skin should be even-coloured and yield slightly to the touch. Be careful to buy ripe fruit, as peaches and nectarines do not continue to ripen – they just go soft. The flesh will be a golden yellow (sometimes with a red blush) or white, depending on variety. Note that clingstone and free-stone varieties refer to whether the fruit is easily removed from the stone.
- Don't buy very hard 'green' fruit, or overripe soft fruit. Avoid fruit with wrinkled and bruised skin.
- Store at room temperature or in the fridge. and use as soon as possible.
- The skin of both is edible, but many people don't like the furry texture of peach skin. It can be removed by blanching (dipping in boiling water) and then putting into cold water, after which it should peel off easily. Either eat in the hand or use in fruit salads and recipes.

Pears

- The new fruit is ready in autumn, but pears are stored in controlled conditions that delay their ripening so that they are available all year round. Choose firm, even-coloured, plump pears with undamaged skin.
- Don't buy soft or bruised pears, or those with brown spots. If they feel soft they are overripe; pears ripen from the inside, so they can be brown and rotten in the centre before the skin betrays any sign that they are past their best.
- Store at room temperature or in the fridge and, once they have softened slightly, use as soon as possible.
- To prepare, wash and dry then eat in the hand or use in recipes. There is no need to peel.

Pineapples

- Buy all year round, choosing fruit that is heavy for its size, yields slightly when pressed and has a sweet aroma. The skin does not have to be golden for the pineapples to be ripe and they don't continue to ripen after picking.
- Don't buy very yellow, soft fruit, especially if the aroma has a hint of fermentation.
- Store in the fridge.
- Prepare by cutting off the top then cutting away the outer scales of the skin. Use a small knife to remove the eyes, then slice into rings or cut into chunks. If the central core is not tough it can be eaten; if it is woody and stringy, discard it.

Plums

- Buy firm, plump, well-coloured plums with unblemished skins which may have a light bloom.
- Don't buy soft fruit, especially if its aroma has a hint of fermentation or if the skin has brown patches. Also avoid hard or shrivelled fruit.
- Store in the fridge and use as soon as possible because plums overripen quickly.
- Eat raw or halve, remove the stone and poach. There is no need to remove the skin.

* Raspberries, strawberries and other berries

- Buy plump, brightly coloured berries that are dry, free from mould and not over-large.
- Don't buy mouldy, squashed and wet fruit, or hard underripe fruit with white patches.
- Store uncovered and unwashed in the fridge and use within a day if possible.
- To prepare, wash and pat dry using absorbent kitchen paper or a clean teatowel. Hull strawberries (remove leaves and stalk).

* Watermelons

- Buy in summer for best bargains. As they are very large, they are often sold in wedges or halves. The flesh should be bright pink.
- Don't buy if the flesh looks wet or soft.
- Store cut pieces in the fridge, wrapped. Whole melons can be stored in a cool, dry, airy place for a week or so.
- Eat in the hand, or with a knife and fork. The black seeds are edible (and far too fiddly to remove, except for special recipes). Alternatively, use a melon baller (Parisienne cutter) or cut into cubes.

Are pesticides worth the risk?

Consumer groups are increasingly worried about the use of chemicals on fruit. Take an orange, for example. Growers spray the fruit after the blossom falls to kill insects and follow this up by almost continuous spraying of pesticides and chemicals to encourage fruit set and growth. After picking it is washed in chlorinated water and sprayed with detergent and post-harvest fungicides before being sprayed with wax to make it look shiny and fresh. The fruit is then cooled and stored in warehouses while it awaits export. On arrival in Britain it may be kept in cold storage again.

There is no requirement to label fruit or vegetables to say what treatments they have undergone or what pesticides and other agro-chemicals have been used on them. The only way to avoid treated fruit and vegetables is to buy produce that is certified 'organic' (that is to say, has been grown without the use of chemicals).

You may be worried that you will increase your intake of pesticides if you eat more fruit and vegetables, but on balance nutritionists think that any potential risk from residues of pesticides is outweighed by the protective effect of fruit and vegetables. Avoiding fruit and vegetables won't remove pesticides from your diet since they are in many other foods. And if you don't eat fruit and vegetables you would probably eat more fatty and sugary foods and we all know what will happen to you then!

How to Eat More Vegetables

There are some very simple ways to eat up more greens without radically changing your diet. Not only will they improve your health, in many cases they'll save money too!

Budget beaters

- Add lots of vegetables to stews and casseroles, especially cheaper root veg such as parsnips, turnips, swede and carrots. Chop the meat into smaller cubes to make it go further.
- Add beans and pulses to stews, casseroles and soups.
- Vegetable and lentil curries are cheap, filling and delicious.
- Cauliflower cheese is popular and easy to make. Cheese sauce can also make a meal of a whole range of vegetables. A dab of mustard allows you to reduce the amount of cheese (and therefore calories) . A small amount of mature cheese goes a lot further than a larger amount of less strongly flavoured cheese.
- Frozen vegetables are sometimes cheaper than fresh, and there is no waste. They retain their nutrients, but don't cook them for too long.

Adding vegetables to ready meals

To cookery enthusiasts it's a sad fact of life that many people prefer to reach for a ready meal than for the raw ingredients to make a meal themselves. However, even keen cooks use ready meals and fast foods occasionally. Many ready meals don't have a portion of vegetables included, so here are some suggestions for choices to make when adding a couple of portions of vegetables to popular ready meals.

- Chilli con carne: Frozen peas, courgettes, grilled tomatoes, salad.
- Lasagne: Frozen peas, broccoli, calabrese, salad.
- Pizza: A green or mixed salad either before or after the pizza.
- Fish fingers: Frozen peas, frozen mixed vegetables, sweetcorn, potatoes.
- Hot pies: Frozen peas, mashed or boiled potatoes, cabbage, carrots, swede.

Takeaways

- Indian: Choose only one meat or fish dish, then make up the rest of the meal by including portions of dahl or other pulse-based dishes and/or vegetable-based dishes. Also include a portion of traditional Indian sambal (the raw, chopped vegetables often served with poppadoms as a starter).
- Chinese: Make your selection as for Indian.
- Fish and chips: Serve with frozen peas or mushy peas and canned tomatoes.
- Burger in a bun and chips: Add a generous portion of salad to the bun, or eat it as a side dish (avoiding the varieties such as burger shop coleslaw, where you get more fatty dressing than salad).
- Fried chicken and chips: Serve with frozen peas, sweetcorn, carrots, green beans.
- Baked potato with cheese or other filling: Serve with a generous portion of salad.

Improving your Sunday roast

- If your family enjoys a Sunday roast, make sure you serve lots of different vegetables (including two varieties of green vegetables) with the roast.
- Minimize the number of roast vegetables – just roast the potatoes, for example. Boil, steam or microwave the others.
- Alternatively, try this method of roasting lamb and vegetables that breaks slightly with tradition. Pierce the skin of the lamb

and insert sprigs of rosemary, then surround the lamb in the roasting pan with a selection of vegetables such as whole baby courgettes or patty pan (mini squash), chunks of red and/or green pepper, quarters of red or Spanish onions, whole tomatoes, chunks of aubergine, peeled cloves of garlic. Briefly blanch the vegetables in a pan of boiling water first, then toss them in a vinaigrette made with 4 tbsp olive oil to 1 tbsp wine vinegar mixed with a tsp each of honey and mustard and chopped herbs of choice. Then arrange around the meat and roast in the usual way, without the addition of any further fat. Serve with boiled (not roast) potatoes.

Chips with anything?

Potatoes are not included in the advice on eating more fruit and vegetables in this chapter because they count as a starchy food, but they are nevertheless a major source of vitamin C in the UK diet – not because they are rich in vitamin C, but because we eat a lot of them.

The best way to cook potatoes is with their skins on (baked, boiled or steamed). If choosing ready-made chips, use thick-cut oven chips rather than thin ones, French fries and other fried potatoes, which are for occasional use only. Avoid chips cooked in saturated fat (i.e. tallow, beef dripping, lard).

Salad All Year Round

Many people think of salad as a summer dish, but in fact it can form part of a healthy diet all year round. Salad needn't consist of the traditional English summer ingredients of lettuce, tomatoes, cucumber – spread your net wider to encompass cooked vegetables, grains and pasta and you'll find you can produce a tasty and filling salad even in mid-winter. Use the following suggestions to start you off on a new way of interpreting the word 'salad', and add fresh chopped herbs whenever they are available.

Spring
● Baby Vegetable Salad: Asparagus, baby carrots, mangetout, baby corn, cherry tomatoes.

- Chinese Salad: Beansprouts, oranges, peanuts, raisins, spring onions or chives, green pepper.
- Tabbouleh: A Middle Eastern classic consisting of cracked wheat (commonly called bulgur or burghul), cooked and mixed with generous amounts of chopped parsley, cucumber, onion or spring onion.
- Salad Niçoise: Cold sliced potato, cold green beans, crispy lettuce, sliced tomatoes, olives, hard-boiled egg, a small amount of chopped tuna and/or anchovies.
- Spinach Salad: Baby (or shredded) spinach leaves tossed with lighter green or red leaves. Add sliced avocado, cold green beans or mangetout and sprinkle generously with chopped fresh herbs.

Summer
- Egg and Bacon Salad: Hard-boiled eggs, mixed salad leaves, garden peas, bacon, young broad beans.
- Potato and Prawn Salad: With plenty of freshly chopped herbs and diced carrot to add crunch.
- Green Bean Salad: Small quantities of tasty sausage or smoked meat, chopped small, served with cold cooked green beans in a light dressing. Vegetarians can sprinkle toasted pine kernels onto the beans instead of meat.
- Tomato Salad: Feta cheese, olives, parsley, spring onions.
- Taco Salad: Fill taco shells with crispy lettuce, chopped onion, tomato, kidney beans, sweetcorn and top with cheese.

Autumn
- Rice salad: With pepper, spring onion, raisins, nuts.
- Pasta salad: Cold cooked pasta shells, sweetcorn, diced peppers, celery, a small amount of chopped tuna or savoury sausage (vegetarians can substitute Edam or Gouda cheese).
- Broccoli Salad: With cashew nuts.
- Carrot, Raisin and Nut Salad.

Winter
- Waldorf Salad: A crisp combination of chopped apple, celery and walnuts served with lettuce (and not too much mayonnaise).

- Bean Salad: Kidney beans, chickpeas, raisins, mushrooms, pepper, onion, celery.
- Pitta Salad Pockets: Chickpeas, raisins, carrots, sunflower seeds, white cabbage, apple.
- Watercress Salad: Watercress, sliced oranges, chicory.
- Mediterranean roast vegetable salads: Oil a baking sheet and quarter, halve or slice any of the following: peppers, fennel, courgettes, tomatoes, onions. Sprinkle with crushed garlic, seasoning, olive oil and chopped basil or parsley. Bake for 20–40 minutes (depending on the hardness of the vegetable) in a moderate oven. Sprinkle with more freshly chopped herbs when cooked. Serve at room temperature.

Salad in sandwiches

The typical British sandwich filling is likely to contain more meat, cheese or fish than salad. Instead, try making the bulk of the sandwich filling vegetable or salad and add a little lean meat, fish or low-fat cheese.

Dentures...

If old age is creeping up on you and dentures make it difficult to eat certain fresh fruit, the best thing to do is to get the dentist to fix your dentures! You should be able to eat these basic foods without trouble. The second-best solution is to chop the fruit up small, as you would if making a fruit salad, and eat it that way. Alternatively, you could process it (skin and all), using a food processor or a juicing attachment, into fresh fruit juice. This can be done with virtually any fruit or vegetable.

... and arthritis

If arthritis makes it difficult on some days to prepare fruit and vegetables, don't peel them! Peeling removes some of their ACE (vitamin and mineral) value and a lot of the fibre, so just wash potatoes, carrots and so on and cook them in their skin. Make use of frozen vegetables and, if you are able to be extravagant, ready-prepared fresh vegetables from supermarkets.

Children's favourites

A lifetime's eating habits are often formed in childhood, so giving children good habits – preferably by example – will help them to enjoy good health in later life. Bribing children to eat vegetables with promises of sugary desserts and sweets will only encourage faddy eating and reinforce the idea that vegetables are horrible.

That said, children do seem to love foods that are not particularly rich in vegetables, so here are some ways to increase the vegetable content of their favourite meals:

- Add grated carrot and chopped celery to mince when making home-made burgers.
- Add brightly coloured vegetables such as peppers, tomatoes and sweetcorn to ready-made pizzas.
- Add diced carrot, peppers and chopped tomatoes to spaghetti bolognese sauce.
- Add sliced and grated vegetables to sandwich fillings (both standard and toasted).
- Serve meat and vegetable kebabs from the barbecue rather than just burgers and sausages without additional vegetables. You can even cut up the burgers and sausages and thread them onto vegetable kebabs.
- Add shredded cabbage, broccoli florets and other vegetables to the mince mixture in shepherd's pie.
- Add swede and carrot to mashed potato.

An A–Z of Every day and ACE Vegetables

= ACE vegetables rich in ACE nutrients

General guidelines

For general guidelines see advice on fruit, pages 56–57.

Aubergines
- Buy glossy, plump, firm vegetables with a smooth skin.
- Don't buy if displaying brown and/or soft spots, or if wrinkled or mouldy around the stem.
- Store in the salad compartment for a week.

- To prepare, wash and dry. Cut immediately before use as the flesh goes brown quickly.

* Beans (green, runner, French, bobby)
- Buy firm, fresh-coloured beans that snap when bent.
- Don't buy blemished, brown, mouldy or floppy, tired-looking beans.
- Store in the salad compartment of the fridge for five days.
- To prepare, wash and trim the top and bottom. Remove the 'strings' from the sides, if necessary. Leave whole or cut into lengths.

Beetroot
- Buy firm, dry roots that feel hard and plump.
- Don't buy bruised, soft, wrinkled, damaged or wet roots.
- Cut off the leaves (but leave some stalk) and store in the salad compartment of the fridge for five days.
- To prepare, peel and grate raw for salads; cook whole in boiling water, steam or cook in a microwave oven or pressure cooker. Remove the skin when cool enough to handle.

Broad beans
- Buy small, tender young pods with a fresh green colour.
- Don't buy large, floppy pods that are sticky from blackfly or marked with brown blemishes.
- Store in the salad compartment of the fridge for a week.
- To prepare, pod the beans when ready to use and boil or steam.

* Broccoli (purple sprouting, calabrese)
- Buy with firm, upright stalks and compact dark green heads.
- Don't buy yellowing heads on floppy stalks.
- Store in the salad compartment of the fridge for a couple of days.
- To prepare, cut large heads into even-sized pieces, using as much stem as possible.

* Brussels sprouts
- Buy small, compact, firm, bright green sprouts.
- Don't buy sprouts with loose yellow leaves, or those that have opened like flowers.

- Store in the salad compartment of the fridge for five days.
- To prepare, trim the stems if necessary and score the bases with a cross to speed cooking. Do not overcook – they should retain some texture, even crispness.

* Cabbages (green, Chinese, white and red, kale, greens)
- Buy firm, crisp cabbage that is heavy for its size.
- Don't buy if the outer leaves are yellowing, soft or coming away from the heart, or if the stalks are floppy.
- Store in the bottom of the fridge in a perforated plastic bag for a week.
- To prepare, break off the outer leaves (green varieties) and wash well in cold water. Discard any yellowing leaves. Cabbage heart may be sliced, but do it just before cooking.

* Carrots
- Buy crisp, firm roots with a good orange colour. If the top is there it should be bright green and fresh.
- Don't buy dry, cracked, dull roots with soft bruised areas or mould around the tops.
- Store in the salad compartment of the fridge for a week.
- To prepare, scrub or scrape in cold water, or peel before grating or cutting into even slices for cooking.

Celery
- Buy compact stalks that are crisp and undamaged.
- Don't buy if the stalks are bruised, browning or limp.
- Store in the salad compartment of the fridge in the plastic bag in which it was packed for a week.
- To prepare, snap stalks off as required and scrub under cold water.

Courgettes and marrows
- Buy firm, dark green vegetables that feel heavy for their size.
- Don't buy shrivelled, soft or bruised vegetables.
- Store in the salad compartment of the fridge for five days.
- To prepare, wash and cut for cooking, removing the seeds from the centre of marrows if liked. There is no need to peel courgettes and tender young marrow.

Cucumber
- Buy firm, fleshy, bright green vegetables.
- Don't buy if soft, dull or damaged.
- Store in the salad compartment of the fridge.
- To prepare, wash and dry before chopping or slicing.

Lettuce, endive and other salad leaves
- Buy firm, fresh-looking lettuce that feels heavy for its size. The crispness of the leaves will depend upon variety. Supermarkets stock interesting ranges of ready-prepared mixed salad leaves.
- Don't buy if the leaves are wilting or going brown, or if the plant feels flimsy or is damaged.
- To store, wash as soon as you get home (see below) and store in the salad compartment of the fridge for four days.
- To prepare, either remove the leaves individually or pull out the heart and wash under cold running water. Drain and dry, using a clean teatowel or salad spinner.

Onions and shallots
- Buy when hard, well-shaped and crisp, with dry, papery skin.
- Don't buy if soft, wet or sprouting.
- Store in a cool, dark, airy and dry place for several weeks.
- To prepare, remove the ends with a sharp knife then pull away the papery skin before slicing.

Parsnips
- Buy small to medium-sized parsnips that are smooth and firm.
- Don't buy if the skin is wrinkled or 'rusted' and the root is soft. Avoid large parsnips as the central core may have become woody.
- Store in a cool, dark, airy and dry place for ten days.
- To prepare, scrub under cold water, peel (optional) and slice or chop as required.

* Peas (garden, mangetout, sugar snap, snow)
- If buying fresh garden peas choose bright green silky pods that look well-filled and firm. The same criteria apply to other types of pea except that some will have flat pods and should break crisply.
- Don't buy if withered and yellowing.

- Store in the salad compartment of the fridge.
- Prepare just before use, either shelling or cooking the pods whole after topping and tailing.

*Peppers

- Buy glossy, crisp and unwrinkled peppers.
- Don't buy if wrinkled, soft, punctured or going mouldy around the stem.
- Store in the salad compartment of the fridge for ten days.
- To prepare, wash and dry, remove the stem and seeds, then use as the recipe requires.

Potatoes

- Buy tubers that are even-sized, firm and smooth, whether they are new or main crop potatoes. Sweet potato should be similarly firm and undamaged. New and salad potatoes should have thin skin.
- Don't buy potatoes with sprouts, scabs, scars or green areas.
- Store main crop and sweet potatoes in a cool, dark, airy place. Don't store new potatoes for more than a day or two in the fridge.
- To prepare, scrub or scrape (there is no need to peel, except for sweet potatoes) and remove any eyes.

*Pumpkins and other types of squash

- Buy hard, heavy-for-size vegetables with a smooth, not-too-thick skin. If buying ready-cut wedges, look for nice bright orange flesh (where appropriate to variety).
- Don't buy if dry, shrivelled or damaged.
- Store whole squash unwrapped in a cool, dry, airy place, where it will keep for several weeks. Store cut pieces in food film in the fridge for five days.
- To prepare, peel varieties with thicker skins or bake in the skin. Remove seeds before using as required.

*Spinach, chard, seakale, beet leaves

- Buy fresh, dark green leaves that look bright and glossy.
- Don't buy wilted, yellowing leaves, or spinach that looks wet and slimy.

- Wash and store in a bag or container in the salad compartment in the fridge and use as soon as possible.
- To prepare, wash the leaves in several changes of cold water and drain well.

* Sprouted seeds
- Buy springy-looking sprouts with a fresh smell.
- Don't buy slimy, wet ones that look limp, brown or stained.
- Store in the fridge for three days in a plastic bag or container, punctured so that the sprouts can breathe.
- To prepare, rinse in cold water, drain well and pat dry on a clean teatowel or absorbent kitchen paper.

Swede and turnips
- Buy hard, crisp roots that are heavy for their size.
- Don't buy shrivelled or damaged roots.
- Store in a cool, dark, airy place or in the fridge.
- To prepare, scrub and peel before using as required.

* Watercress
- Buy whole bunches in preference to those that are ready-trimmed and washed. Choose glossy, dark green leaves and firm stalks.
- Don't buy yellowing or flowering cress.
- To store, wash and dry as for lettuce before storing for a couple of days.
- Prepare as for lettuce.

Cook's tips for preserving ACE vitamins and minerals

- Eating some raw fruits and vegetables helps boost your nutrient intake as cooking destroys vitamins.
- Beta carotene is stable during mild heating, but losses occur at high temperatures.
- Vitamin C and beta carotene leach out during cooking because they are water-soluble – so if you throw the cooking water down the sink you will lose some of the nutrients.

What's left of the vitamin C after cooking?

	% of vitamin C retained after cooking
Whole green beans, boiled	54
Cut green beans, boiled	28
Broccoli, steamed or stir-fried	78
Broccoli boiled, covered with water in an uncovered pan	45
Potatoes, peeled, boiled and mashed	50–70
Potatoes, baked, boiled unpeeled, steamed	60–80
Chips	65–75

As these figures show, the more you do to fruit and vegetables the greater the vitamin loss.

- Vitamin E is stable in cooking but is oxidized (destroyed) by contact with the air. Overheating and overuse of cooking oils also destroys vitamin E.

The way to minimize vitamin loss is:

1. Cook for the shortest possible time.
2. Cook in the minimum amount of water. Add food to boiling water. Better still, steam, microwave or use a waterless cooker.
3. Prepare immediately before cooking.
4. Don't chop fruit and vegetables too small because that exposes more surfaces for nutrient loss.
5. Tear the leaves of green leafy vegetables rather than cutting them with a knife
6. Dress cut fruit and vegetables in lemon juice to prevent vitamin C loss by oxidation.

The way to minimize mineral loss is:

1. Use cooking water for soups, sauces and so on because cooking doesn't destroy minerals – they just leach out into the cooking water.

Serving food

1. Serve immediately after cooking as more losses occur if food is kept warm or reheated.
2. Serve the cooking liquid if possible in soups or sauces.
3. Avoid further processing such as mashing or puréeing.

Aluminium pans and Alzheimer's disease

As yet cause and effect has not been conclusively proved between aluminium in the diet and Alzheimer's disease, but the use of aluminium pans has been linked to Alzheimer's for several reasons. Concentrations of aluminium appear in the tangles in the brain that characterize the disease; cases are 50 per cent higher in areas where natural aluminium levels in the water are high; and drugs that reduce the aluminium content of the brain have slowed the progress of the disease.

Anyone who has cooked fruit in an aluminium pan will have noticed that it has the effect of scouring the pans so that they are bright and shiny. The citrate in the fruit erodes the coating and makes the aluminum more readily absorbable. While this can't be said to cause Alzheimer's disease, it is at least certain that cooking fruit in glass or stainless steel pans will not cause you to ingest aluminium!

CHAPTER 5

How ACE Eating Fits Into a Healthy Diet and Lifestyle

Eating more fruit and vegetables to boost your energy and immune system and reduce your risk of cancer and heart disease sounds – and is – easy enough. But what else, if anything, do you need to do? Do you carry on as normal in all other respects? Well, that depends on what you regard as 'normal'. So, let's see if your food intake matches up to what experts worldwide now agree is the healthiest diet.

Five steps to the healthiest diet

1. Eat at least five portions of fruit and vegetables a day. Especially good are green and yellow fruit and vegetables and citrus fruit.
2. Eat half your diet as starchy foods like cereals, breads, potatoes, rice and other grains.
3. The rest of your diet (for non-vegetarians) should include relatively low amounts of lean meat, poultry or low-fat dairy produce, with fish two or three times a week instead of meat.
4. Go easy on alcohol, salt and sugar.
5. Go easy on pickled, smoked and salt-preserved foods.

These five steps will also help to control weight problems without you going hungry, for if you fill up on the foods described there will be less need for confectionery, biscuits and other fatty foods.

Fruit and vegetables

In the UK we eat about 250g/8oz of fruit and vegetables a day. We should double that to at least 400g/14 oz a day (which excludes potatoes, as they are starchy foods). You need to include 30g/1oz a day of pulses, nuts and seeds if you are a vegetarian (though this is beneficial for everyone). This adds up to about five portions a day, which is easy to fit into a perfectly 'normal' diet. For example:

- Have a glass of fruit juice for breakfast (one portion).
- Eat an apple or another portion of fruit as a snack during the day – each piece of fruit counts as one portion (see fruit list in Chapter 4).
- At the main meal of the day eat two portions of vegetables (fresh, frozen or canned), excluding potatoes (see Chapter 4 for typical portion sizes).
- At one meal of the day have a fruit-based pudding, which counts as another portion.

Total: 5 portions a day – without really trying!

Starchy foods

In the UK we eat 27 per cent of our calories as starchy foods. We need to increase that to about 50 per cent of calories. For most people, reaching that target means doubling the amount of bread, potatoes and cereals. Contrary to popular belief, starchy foods like bread, potatoes and pasta are not fattening – it's the fat that is added during and after cooking and piled on bread that boosts up the calories.

People are sometimes confused about what is meant by carbohydrates or starchy foods. There are two main types of carbohydrate:

Complex carbohydrates (starchy foods) – EAT MORE
These are starchy foods such as cereals, bread, pasta, potatoes, pulses, whole grains, fruit and vegetables. Dietary fibre was previously thought to be the magic ingredient but we now know that whole starchy foods are more valuable because they also contain vitamins and minerals which work in combination with fibre.

Simple carbohydrates (free sugars) – EAT LESS
This is what you and I would call 'sugar', whether it has been refined from sugar cane or beet and whether it is added to food at home or eaten as an ingredient of processed foods such as cakes, biscuits and pastries. 'Free sugars' also includes other disguises for sugar such as glucose syrup, honey and so on.

Fibre

On average we each eat 21g/¾oz of fibre a day, which we should aim to increase to around 27g/1oz (although you can go up to 40g/1½oz).
While many people eat high-fibre foods such as breakfast cereals to avoid constipation there are other substances in fibre (especially the fibre found in oats, beans, barley, rye, vegetables and some fruit) that also help to lower blood cholesterol.

In fact, there are dozens of different types of fibre in starchy foods – for example, gums, pectin and other substances resistant to digestion – that work together with ACE nutrients to protect health. Eating lots of starchy foods and five portions of fruit and vegetables a day means you won't need to add bran to your food. Too much bran can result in a loss of minerals such as iron, zinc and calcium which are bound up by substances called phytates in bran and made unavailable to the body.

For more information about fibre, see Appendix II, page 188.

Sugar

In the British diet 13 per cent of calories currently come from sugar. We should try to reduce that amount by about a third. In fact, you don't need to eat any sugar for energy, as starchy foods are digested to give the body all the energy it needs and there are also sugars in milk and fruit. Nevertheless, most people enjoy sweet things and don't want to give them up entirely. If this applies to you, at least try to keep them to a minimum.

Fats

About 40 per cent of our calories come from fat, and our goal should be 30 per cent or less. While we have known for a long time that we eat too much fat we haven't changed our habits –

perhaps because we have not known what to eat instead! Now we know that the bulk of the diet should be fruit and vegetables and starchy foods it should be easier to do.

Eating too many fatty foods, especially those high in saturated fats, can raise blood cholesterol levels. This increases the risk of a build-up of cholesterol in the artery walls, making them narrower and slowing down the supply of blood to the heart – or even cutting it off completely, at which point a heart attack occurs.

Cutting down on fat is not the whole answer. As we have seen, ACE nutrients in fruit and vegetables are protective, but as coronary heart disease has many causes it is also important not to smoke, to take enough exercise, and to learn to cope with stress. Most importantly, if you have raised blood pressure work on lowering it.

Saturated fats
We eat 16 per cent of our calories as saturated fat – mainly animal fats and hydrogenated (hardened) vegetable oils – when we should be eating no more than 10 per cent.

Polyunsaturated fats
We eat 6 per cent of calories as polyunsaturates (vegetable and fish fats and oils), which is fine because we don't need, and indeed shouldn't eat, any more than 10 per cent. Polyunsaturated fats have been shown to help reduce blood cholesterol levels, but there is an upper limit because studies on animals suggest that eating too much (especially if you don't eat enough vitamin E), might increase the risk of certain cancers through free-radical formation. (Cold-pressed extra-virgin olive oil does itself contain vitamin E, as does sunflower oil and some of its products, but in some vegetable oils the vitamin will have been destroyed in the processing.) However, there is not enough evidence to prove that polyunsaturates have been associated with human disease. It has been suggested that, if eaten in large quantities, polyunsaturates may also lower the beneficial type of cholesterol as well as the harmful type.

Monounsaturated fats
The richest sources of monounsaturated fat are olive, peanut and rapeseed oils, but the main sources in the UK diet are meat and milk, simply because they form a large part of our diet. (They are

also, of course, responsible for most of the saturated fat we con-sume.) Like polyunsaturates, monounsaturates can help to lower blood cholesterol. They may have an advantage over polyunsatu-rates in not decreasing the good type of cholesterol as much. In general the advice is to keep them at the current level of around 12 per cent of calories. If you are thinking of switching to olive oil it should replace saturated fats, not be in addition to them, and be part of a low-fat diet.

Trans fats

Having got used to the idea that saturated fats are bad for us and polyunsaturates and monounsaturates are good, we now have another type of fat to contend with: trans fats. We eat about 5g a day, which is 2 per cent of calories, and it's recommended that we don't eat any more because, like saturated fats, trans fats seem to raise blood cholesterol and tip the balance of cholesterol away from the good type towards the harmful type.

You won't see trans fats mentioned in the nutritional labelling on food packaging because they are not usually measured and there is no provision in labelling regulations for them. The main source is margarine, particularly the hard type, as they are pro-duced when vegetable oils are hydrogenated (hardened) to turn them into cooking and spreading fats. Good quality soft spreads and margarines contain around the same amount of trans fats as butter.

Fish oils

The type of polyunsaturates found in fish oils can help to make blood less likely to clot, reducing the risk of coronary heart dis-ease. Fish oils also lower levels of harmful fats, but it is not clear how much this helps to prevent coronary heart disease. Replac-ing meat at least twice a week with fish helps to replace saturated fats with unsaturated fats, while white fish is also high in vita-mins and minerals. Obviously, to gain the full benefit from fish it has to be a regular part of your diet.

How to cut down on sugar and fat

If all this talk about the problems with fat has you declaring a fat-free existence, think again. You can't cut out fat altogether – you need to eat some polyunsaturated fat because it is an essential nutrient that the body can't make.

However, you may well need to reduce the amount of fat you eat – but if you are cutting down on fat don't make the common mistake of filling up on sugar, and vice versa. (Studies of the way we eat show that people who cut down on sugars eat more fats and so increase their risk of heart disease.) And don't feel you are depriving yourself because healthier eating is not about going without, it's about making the best choices – and that means replacing fatty and sugary foods with fruit and vegetables and starchy foods.

Go nuts now and again

Fats in nuts are mainly unsaturated (except for macadamia and coconut) and nuts could replace some meat in your diet – especially since an American study has demonstrated that 84g/3½oz of walnuts a day, eaten instead of other fatty foods, reduced harmful types of cholesterol and increased amounts of good cholesterol. Although the study used 84g/3½oz, in fact 28g/1oz also gives positive results. But don't go mad because nuts are still high-fat, and therefore high-calorie, foods.

Know your cheese

Low-fat cheese (with 25 per cent or fewer calories from fat)
- Fromage frais, quark and similar low-fat soft white cheese (check labels as there are also higher-fat versions)

Medium-fat cheese (with 45 per cent or fewer calories from fat)
- Cottage cheese (35 per cent)

High-fat cheese (with 60 per cent or more calories from fat)
- Cheddar and other hard cheeses
- Blue cheeses
- Cream cheeses
- Edam

- Brie
- Camembert
- Goat's cheese

Know your meat and fish

Low fat – may be eaten often
- White fish – poached or steamed
- Roast chicken and turkey – no skin
- Lean roast beef
- Canned fish in brine
- Prawns
- Scallops
- Game, such as venison
- Lean roast leg port
- Trout (grilled or steamed)

Medium fat – may be eaten quite often
- Lean boiled ham
- Lean roast duck – no skin
- Lean roast leg of lamb
- Stewed offal
- Sardines and pilchards in tomato sauce
- Lean grilled pork chop – no fat
- Stewed rabbit
- Lean beef

Medium-high fat – eat only occasionally and in small quantities
- Bacon
- Mince (except lean mince)
- Chops
- Gammon – meat and fat
- Liver sausage
- Sausages
- Salami
- Luncheon meat
- Meat pies
- Pâté
- Scotch egg

Salt

We eat about 9g/¼oz of salt a day, which is equivalent to 4g/⅛oz sodium. We need less than half that amount. Lowering sodium intake could be of benefit in reducing high blood pressure and heart disease in susceptible people, especially as there is a relationship between sodium intake and a rise in blood pressure as we age. Most people eat twice the amount they need because so much is added to processed foods, which account for three-quarters of the salt we ingest – another good reason for preparing your own fresh, unprocessed food.

Protein

Generally speaking, as long as you eat enough calories you will eat enough protein. Even in countries where cereals and pulses are the main foods eaten (which means in most of the world), those who have enough to eat obtain sufficient protein for health. We often forget that vegetables provide protein because we think of protein only in terms of meat, fish and dairy produce. Yet as part of a varied diet, plant foods provide 10–15 per cent of calories in the form of protein.

Vegetarians are advised to combine different sources of vegetable protein. These are 1) beans and pulses; 2) nuts and seeds; 3) cereals and grains. And for vegetarians who eat dairy produce such as milk, cheese and yogurt, mixing these foods with the three groups above increases the amount of protein available.

Watching your weight?

1 gram of carbohydrates (sugar and starch) provides
    3.75 calories
1 gram of fat provides 9 calories
1 gram of alcohol provides 7 calories
1 gram of protein provides 4 calories

Smoked food and ACE nutrients

Nitrites are chemicals used to help preserve some smoked and pickled foods such as smoked fish and bacon. In the stomach they may be turned into nitrosamines, substances that can promote cancer. Stomach cancer is more common in populations where lots of smoked, pickled and salt-preserved foods are eaten and low in countries where lots of fresh fruit and vegetables and small amounts of smoked foods are eaten. In Japan, where lots of vegetables and smoked and salty food are consumed, stomach cancer is common. The missing protective factor in the Japanese diet is probably fruit, especially citrus fruit. Vitamins E and C may prevent the conversion of nitrites to nitrosamines in the stomach. (There is also less stomach cancer nowadays because refrigeration means less reliance on pickled foods.)

Meat and vitamin E

While meat contains useful vitamins and minerals it doesn't contain any vitamin C or beta carotene and the vitamin E content is depleted or destroyed by freezing. Extra vitamin E is sometimes added to meat to keep its colour and extend the shelf life, but it isn't really enough to make a contribution to your ACE nutrients. The diet of beef cattle is being supplemented with vitamin E in experimental beef rearing to see if it will produce redder, more cosmetically pleasing meat with a longer shelf life.

To drink or not to drink

Moderate drinking (two drinks a day) as part of a healthy, traditional Mediterranean-style diet rich in fruit and vegetables is associated with a longer, healthier life. Of course this doesn't mean that everyone should start drinking alcohol. That is unlikely ever to become 'official' advice, not least because it would encourage those who already drink to increase their consumption and drink too much – and don't forget that in France, where the low rate of heart disease is attributed to the consumption of wine, large numbers of people die of liver disease such as cirrhosis and cancer of the mouth and throat, also linked to their alcohol consumption.

What it does mean is that if those moderate drinkers who take around two units of alcohol a day (i.e. about 21 per cent of British men and 14 per cent of British women) stick to the 'safe levels' (no more than 21 units a week for men and 14 for women), spread their drinking out evenly rather than binging and have a couple of alcohol-free days a week they can carry on enjoying themselves – and at the same time get protection against coronary heart disease, some cancers (see page 34) and other health problems.

The exception to this is pregnant women (or women who are likely to be pregnant but are not as yet confirmed to be so), who should not drink any alcohol at all until they reach the fourth month of pregnancy, when current wisdom allows one or two drinks a week thereafter.

Incidentally, the protection offered by alcohol is over and above that gained from eating more fruit and vegetables and following a generally healthy diet and lifestyle.

Units of alcohol

As a general rule, one unit of alcohol equals the following:

1 pub measure (⅙th gill/25ml/1fl oz) of spirits (Scottish pub spirit measures are 1.2 units)
1 small (80ml/2¾fl oz) glass of sherry or other fortified wine
1 small (125ml/4fl oz) glass of wine
300ml/½ pint ordinary beer, lager or cider
125ml/¼ pint strong beer, lager or cider
2 small (125ml/4fl oz) glasses low-alcohol wine
900ml/1½ pints low-alcohol beer, lager or cider

Cigarettes

For many people a cigarette automatically accompanies a drink but there is nothing to recommend smoking, which causes lung cancer and heart disease and is a hazard to 'passive' smokers – those in proximity to smokers who inhale sidestream cigarette smoke.

Extra ACE nutrients and B vitamins are needed by the body to cope with the toxins that result from smoking. However, diet surveys show that smokers generally eat less fruit and vegetables and other nutrient-rich foods than non-smokers, even though their habit demands a greater intake of vitamins and minerals.

Interestingly, in Japan, where smoking rates are high, coronary heart disease rates are lower than might be expected. Some scientists suggest this may be due to relatively high ACE vitamin and mineral intake that could be protective against the harmful effects of smoking. However, eating lots of antioxidant vitamins and minerals does *not* mean you can smoke without risk of coronary heart disease.

Antioxidants as food additives

Antioxidants, including ACE nutrients such as vitamin C (ascorbic acid) E300 and vitamin E (tocopherols) E306, are used in foods to prevent them going rancid. Beta carotene E160(a) is used in food as a colouring. Both 'natural' and synthetic versions of vitamin C E301, E302, E304 and vitamin E E307, E308, E309 are used as food additives. Foods which contain these additives don't necessarily give you extra ACE protection because the quantities used are small and are designed only to protect the nutrients in the food or stop it discolouring.

Seven-day eating plan

Before you start, remember the five-a-day rule: Each day include at least five portions of fruit and/or vegetables in your diet. To meet the target add portions of vegetables and servings of salad to the suggestions for lunch and evening meals given below. See Chapter 4 for fruit and vegetables rich in ACE nutrients.

Breakfast

Each day include fresh fruit juice or a piece of fresh or dried fruit with your breakfast. Use skimmed milk with cereal and choose low-fat and low-sugar breakfast cereals. Limit traditional cooked British breakfasts (except porridge) to once or twice a week.

Lunch

Follow the suggestions given on pages 88–91 with a piece of fresh fruit or a low-fat fruit yogurt or fromage frais if you want a 'pudding' with your lunch.

Snacks

The eating plan below does not include snacks. If you feel the need for between-meals bites, choose fruit, raw vegetables, wholemeal sandwiches, wholemeal buns, wholemeal scones or other low-fat and low-sugar baked items, low-fat yogurt or other low-fat dairy products such as fromage frais.

Day 1

Breakfast
Fruit juice
Granola (page 178) with skimmed milk and fresh fruit
Wholemeal toast with polyunsaturated sunflower spread rich in vitamin E

Lunch
Stuffed peppers (page 120)
Baked potato(es)

Dinner
Salmon fishcakes with salsa verde (page 155)
Salad
Vegetarian alternative
Salad tacos (page 115)
Baked potato(es)
Poached fruit salad (page 159)

Day 2

Breakfast
Fruit juice
Raisin bread (page 176)
Breakfast cereal (see page 87)

Lunch
Lentil and apricot soup (page 109)
Wholemeal bread

Dinner
Gammon steaks with curried fruit (page 140)
Brown rice or potatoes
Vegetarian alternative
Vegetable risotto (page 127)
Fruity bread and butter pudding (page 162)

Day 3

Breakfast
Fruit juice
Choice from Day 1 or Day 2 or see note on page 87

Lunch
Broccoli quiche (page 118)
Salad
Potatoes or wholemeal bread

Dinner
Vegetable chop suey (page 133)
Brown rice
Tricolour melon salad with blackcurrant coulis (page 163)

Day 4

Breakfast
Fruit juice
Choice from Day 1 or Day 2 or see note on page 87

Lunch
Eggs en piperade (page 124)
Wholemeal bread

Dinner
Chicken and chorizo paella (page 146)
Salad
Vegetarian alternative
Courgette bake (page 130)
Salad
Apple strudel (page 165)

Day 5

Breakfast
Fruit juice
Choice from Day 1 or Day 2 or see note on page 87

Lunch
Red pepper and tomato soup (page 111)
Wholemeal bread
Salad

Dinner
Stuffed aubergines (page 141)
Ratatouille (page 121)

Vegetarian alternative
Aubergine cannelloni (page 136)
Salad
Poached apricots (page 161)

Day 6

Breakfast
Fruit juice
Choice from Day 1 or Day 2 or see note on page 87

Lunch
Flat bean and salami salad (page 114)
Wholemeal bread

Vegetarian alternative
Gado gado (page 116)

Dinner
Grilled tuna with red salsa (page 154)

Vegetarian alternative
Spinach gnocchi with tomato sauce (page 126)
Salad
Pumpkin pie (page 158)

Day 7

Breakfast
Fruit juice
Choice from Day 1 or Day 2 or see note on page 87

Lunch
Pissaladière (page 123)
Salad

Dinner
Poussin provençale (page 139)

Vegetarian alternative
Provençale pie (page 134)
Hot fruit salad (page 164)

CHAPTER 6

Is ACE Eating Enough?

While there is plenty of general advice about eating more fruit and vegetables and growing acceptance of the concept of optimal nutrition, there is very little agreement on the exact quantities of antioxidant ACE nutrients we need. This is mainly because the research has not yet been done to define and measure optimal nutrition, and how ACE eating achieves it.

There is also debate about whether we need only the amount of vitamins and minerals recommended by the government, whose figures are based on sufficient to prevent deficiency diseases (see Table 17, page 93), or whether we need to obtain a lot more for so-called 'optimal health', a state which, theoretically, slows down ageing and protects us against heart disease, cancer, cataracts, and so on. Indeed, some experts have argued that if antioxidant nutrients can protect us against cancer and heart disease then these (and other) diseases could be seen as deficiency diseases caused by low intake of ACE nutrients. Until all the research work has been done, however, that remains only a theory.

ACE for optimal health

To have the lowest risk of disease (as opposed to avoiding deficiencies) Professor Anthony Diplock, Head of Biochemistry at Guy's and St Thomas's Medical School, London, suggests the following intake of antioxidant nutrients, which is much higher than the government recommendations:

Beta-carotene: 15–25mg/day.

Vitamin E: 50–80mg/day; higher levels necessary to counteract high polyunsaturated fat content of some people's diet.

Vitamin C: 100–150mg a day.

These figures are based on existing evidence of the protective role of antioxidants against chronic disease (heart disease, certain cancers and inflammatory diseases such as rheumatoid arthritis). Other researchers and nutritionists go further and recommend up to 1g a day of vitamin C and 150–200mg of vitamin E.

What's the best way of getting ACE nutrients?

Whether you decide you need the minimum amount of ACE nutrients or the maximum for optimal nutrition, there are still questions to be considered – namely, is it best to obtain ACE nutrients from food or from dietary supplements? And can sufficient ACE nutrients be obtained from food alone?

From the typical day's eating charts below, the bottom line seems to be that you can get enough vitamin C and beta carotene to match the likely optimum nutrition levels if you choose your food wisely (though most people don't). However, it's virtually impossible to get the very high amounts of vitamin E recommended by some without eating a lot of fat.

The examples that follow on pages 95–96 look at each vitamin separately, mainly so that you can focus on foods rich in those ACE nutrients, but there will be a certain amount of all ACE nutrients in each menu – and as ACE nutrients work together in the body they are all important.

Table 17: Summary of the British government's Reference Nutrient Intakes of ACE vitamins (plus folic acid)

Age	Folic acid mcg/day	Vitamin C mg/day	*Vitamin A mcg/day
0–3 months	50	25	350
4–6 months	50	25	350
7–9 months	50	25	350
10–12 months	50	25	350
1–3 years	70	30	400
4–6 years	100	30	500
7–10 years	150	30	500
Males			
11–14 years	200	35	600
15–18 years	200	40	700
19–50 years	200	40	700
51–64 years	200	40	700
65 + years	200	40	700
Females			
11–14 years	200	35	600
15–18 years	200	40	700
19–50 years	200	40	700
50–64 years	200	40	700
65+ years	200	40	700
Pregnancy	100*	10	100
Lactation	60	30	350

* Vitamin A = retinol, the ready-formed vitamin A in animal foods, and retinol equivalents, the beta carotene found in plant foods and converted to retinol in the body.

Beta carotene and vitamin E are not listed in the above chart because the British government feels it does not yet have enough data to set intakes. However, EC Labelling Directives, which cover UK food products, have set an RDA of 10 mg vitamin E a day.

The American government, however, has a recommended daily amount for vitamin E (22mg a day for men and 18mg a day for women), but no recommendation for beta carotene.

Beta carotene

To eat 15–25mg of beta carotene – the amount that might be needed for optimal health – a typical day's diet might include the following foods.

Breakfast	*Approx mg beta carotene*
Dried fruit compote (prunes, apricots, peaches etc.) and yogurt	0.50 mg
Toast spread with butter or fortified margarine/spread	0.08 mg
125ml/¼ pint glass orange juice	0.20 mg
Lunch	
Poached salmon/trout	
sandwiches including 50g/2oz watercress	1.50 mg
125ml/¼ pint glass tomato juice	0.20 mg
150g/5oz Cantaloupe melon	1.50 mg
Afternoon snack	
Slice of pumpkin pie	1.50 mg
Main meal	
Lean meat or fish or vegetarian equivalent served with	
75g/3oz boiled carrots	6.00 mg
80g/3¼oz spinach	3.00 mg
Fruit salad containing ¼ mango, 2 fresh apricots and 1 orange	3.20 mg
Total	17.68 mg

Vitamin C

To eat 100–150 mg a day of vitamin C – the amount that might be needed for optimum health – a day's diet might include the following foods.

Breakfast	*Approx mg vitamin C*
Half a grapefruit and toast with marmalade	40.00 mg
Lunch	
Crudités (raw vegetables) including green pepper, carrots	
with hummus or similar dip	60.00 mg
125ml/¼ pint glass orange juice	48.00 mg
Afternoon snack	
1 apple	3.00 mg
Main meal	
Vegetable stir fry including peppers,	
carrots, beansprouts, served with rice	100.00 mg
Blackcurrant crumble	15.00 mg
Total	266.00 mg

Vitamin E

It is very difficult to eat sufficient vitamin E in a day. According to Professor Diplock, the amount that might be needed for optimal health is 50–80 mg (equivalent to 75–120 international units) and even in a day's diet that was rich in a variety of foods that are natural sources of vitamin E (see below) you would not come near that total.

	Approx mg vitamin E
Breakfast	
Muesli and wholemeal toast or bread with margarine/ spread fortified with vitamin E	6.00 mg
Lunch	
100g/4oz tuna in oil with large green mixed salad dressed with sunflower vinaigrette	8.60 mg
Afternoon snack	
Slice of fruit cake	1.10 mg
Main meal	
Half an avocado, followed by vegetable risotto (page 127) and blackberry crumble	12.00 mg
Total	27.70 mg

However, if you were to include recipes using sunflower spread enriched with vitamin E you could achieve 50 mg a day. To do so the following changes could be made to the above:

Lunch
Add 2 slices of wholemeal bread spread with a vitamin-E rich spread.

Afternoon snack
Swap the fruit cake for a slice of carrot cake (page 173).

Main meal
Swap the risotto for spicy meat peppers (page 145).
Swap the crumble for apple and blackberry pie (page 171).

The perils of modern living

If you think it seems strange that 'nature' has put us in a situation in which we require higher levels of vitamins and minerals than are available from food, there is the possibility that modern, man-made events have increased our needs for vitamins and minerals. Air pollution, cigarette smoke, X-rays, holes in the ozone layer that increase UV radiation, drugs, chemicals and toxins that enter the food and water chain, food additives and food refining all contribute to what is probably an increased need for ACE nutrients to combat the ravages of free-radical (oxidative) damage.

You have probably heard some people say that taking vitamin pills is a waste of money if you are apparently healthy; it just produces very expensive urine (because excess of some vitamins is expelled from the body in this way). But just because you don't have any clinical or outward sign of deficiency – such as scurvy or rickets – it doesn't mean that you are eating enough ACE nutrients to protect you against heart disease and cancer, or even that you are nourished enough to feel good. While there are theories about ACE nutrients that are as yet unproven, the tide of opinion now seems to be turning in favour of better nutrition, partly because of hard economic facts. The cost of the pursuit of 'cure-all' medicines and magic bullet drugs that has dominated the medical profession since the discovery of antibiotics and other drugs that can kill infections is now so great that high-tech, drug-led medicine has become too expensive, resulting in rationing within the NHS and forcing a re-evaluation of the importance of preventive medicine. This has become even more vital as the human lifespan increases and the nation has to spend more and more to maintain people in their (sick) old age.

Cataracts are a good example of this. With an ageing population more and more cataract operations are needed, so researchers are looking for ways to prevent cataracts, or at least delay their onset by around ten years. It's estimated that this will halve costs, because such operations are usually done on people who live less than ten years afterwards.

Economic necessities have coincided with the 'second wave' of nutritional science. The first was the discovery of vitamins and the deficiency diseases, which was just getting underway when the medical world went 'drugs-mad', relegating nutrition to secondary (if any) interest. It never became part of the curriculum in medical schools, for example, and today is only taught in a limited way in some of them. Only now is the possibility that we may need greater amounts of nutrients for optimal health and the prevention of chronic diseases being taken seriously, because it's a serious money-saving investment.

We haven't yet reached the point at which there is a simple test that shows how much damage has been done to our bodies by free-radical damage and allows doctors to prescribe ACE nutrients to prevent people developing serious diseases. While one may not be that far off, with measurement of the level of malondialdehyde (a stable final product of oxidation found in the urine) possibly being the best single measurement, it will probably never be an over-the-counter quick test.

Where does this leave you?

You now know that you can get the recommended amounts of beta carotene and vitamin C from your daily diet and the recommended amounts of vitamin E if you include enriched foods such as sunflower spread. But is it better to get them from pills? And can you get away with eating a junk diet if you take dietary supplements?

Some studies suggest taking pills is better than relying on your diet. Taking beta-carotene supplements, for example, increases the amount of beta carotene circulating in the blood more effectively than eating cooked carrots, cooked broccoli or drinking tomato juice.

But that's not the whole story, because while beta-carotene levels increase, levels of other carotenoids found alongside beta carotene in food that are probably also important for health actually decrease. This means that vitamin supplements might upset the natural balance of nutrients obtained from foods. Foods high in carotenoids may also contribute other biologically active substances that are not present in purified vitamin or mineral supplements. These other constituents may be important for decreasing cancer risk and contributing to better health.

Consequently, pills are probably not as good as food, although they may turn out to be necessary for 'topping up' on ACE nutrients. While scientists say that vitamin C is the same whether it comes in an orange or is made in the factory laboratory and taken as a pill, there's no denying that a pill doesn't contain all the other ingredients in food, the importance of which is not yet known. Scientists have yet to understand the role of the obscure ingredients such as the substances in cabbages thought to protect against cancer, and the phenols, luteins, flavones and so on. These natural combinations of ACE nutrients and other substances found with them in foods may be jointly responsible for the protective effect of foods rich in ACE nutrients.

Surveys by consumer groups have shown that not all dietary supplements deliver what they promise. Some do not contain the amount of nutrients stated; others do not dissolve in the body so that the nutrients can be properly digested. However, when they work they are probably no worse at delivering ACE nutrients than eating up your greens.

You do need supplements...

According to Professor Diplock, who has spent 35 years doing research on vitamin E and selenium, supplementation is the last resort, but is probably necessary. While improving the diet should be the first step, Professor Diplock thinks there is serious doubt as to whether the levels of antioxidant nutrients needed to give optimal protection against disease can be obtained through diet alone. He says:

'We are by no means at the point where a cause and effect relationship between vitamin E intake and disease prevention has been proved but, if the case turns out to be proven completely, then food fortification is likely to be the way forward. In the interim, however, it is difficult to achieve even 50 international units from diet alone and so I believe we should encourage people to take a modest natural supplement, particularly one as safe as vitamin E.'

Other researchers and nutritionists, especially those working in America, go further than Professor Diplock's recommendations and suggest 200–500 mg a day of vitamin C and 150–200 mg of vitamin E – amounts that have been used in research. They also recommend supplements of zinc, selenium and folic acid (folate).

However, not everyone is in agreement.

You don't need supplements

The *British Medical Journal*, a scientific journal for doctors, takes the view that you don't need supplements. Leader writers say, firstly, that people eating a good diet are more likely to take them than those at risk of nutrient deficiency; secondly, that the vitamins people choose to take are often not the ones inadequate in their diet; and thirdly, people may not know what dose they need and toxic effects have been established for mega-doses of vitamin B6 (pyridoxine), and the fat-soluble vitamins A and D. In short, says the *BMJ*, 'All too often the wrong people are taking the wrong doses of the wrong vitamins.'

What are the risks of overdosing on ACE vitamins?

Vitamin A

There is a danger of overdosing on this vitamin (which is not, strictly speaking, an antioxidant). That is why pregnant women have been advised not to eat liver or take vitamin A pills (see page 103). In other people, more than 7,500mcg (36 times the RNI for men, 40 for women) can result in liver damage, hair loss, blurred vision, bone damage and headaches (as the Arctic explorers who died after existing on polar bear liver proved).

Beta carotene

Heard the one about the health food freak who ate pounds of carrots a day and turned orange? Well, it's true – excessive amounts of carrot juice or carrots can turn the palms of the hands and soles of the feet orange (that's why beta carotene has been used in self-tanning tablets). However, there is no danger from beta-carotene; it is non-toxic and any excess will be dealt with harmlessly by the body.

Vitamin C

You'll know when you have taken too large a dose of vitamin C because you will develop diarrhoea. Usually, an excess of vitamin C is simply lost in the urine. People who have been taking a lot over a period of time have scurvy-like symptoms when the dose is reduced, but they soon get back to normal. There may be some danger of kidney stones for people taking too much vitamin C.

Vitamin E

A number of studies have shown that vitamin E is safe to take even in quite large doses. For example, in trials where daily intake was 894–47,680 mg (the US RDA is 22 mg for men and 18 mg for women per day) for up to six months very few side effects were observed and none was consistently seen. The experts who advised the British government on the amounts it is safe to eat (see Appendix I) also said few adverse effects were reported on up to 32,000 mg a day, and none consistently. This amount is probably 10 times that needed to prevent oxidative damage.

Warning: if you are taking medicine for heart disease, such as blood-thinning drugs, consult your doctor before taking vitamin E as it might interfere with the treatment.

What are the risks of overdosing on ACE minerals ?

Copper

There is only a small amount of information about the need for copper, but it is a component of antioxidant enzymes. High intakes are harmful; this is not a problem in the UK but can be in other parts of the world where water is contaminated with copper. More research is needed on the role of copper in the body, especially as people with high blood cholesterol and those who have had heart attacks have raised levels. Copper is also a potent pro-oxidant (see page 36).

Manganese

The safe intakes set for this mineral are 1.4 mg a day in adults and 16mcg per kilogram of body weight a day in children and adolescents. Manganese is one of the least toxic of all elements. If too much is eaten it is excreted via bile and kidneys.

Selenium

This mineral is essential for free radical-busting enzymes. There are recommended intakes, but not enough is known about how much we need. Selenium is toxic and so the upper intake has been set at 6 mcg per kilogram of body weight per day in adults.

Zinc

This is another essential mineral for making protective enzymes. There are recommended intakes, and too much zinc interferes with the absorption of other minerals such as calcium. Eating 2g a day produces nausea and vomiting and long-term intakes of 50 mg a day interfere with the body's use of copper.

Problems with iron

Iron deficiencies can leave you tired and vulnerable to infection, but if you are not anaemic taking iron supplements may not be a good idea because iron can encourage the formation of free radicals. It has even been suggested that British women's low iron status might be a blessing in disguise by protecting them against heart disease!

One third of menstruating women (aged 11–50) in northern Europe are reported to have no iron stores. After the menopause iron stores accumulate and this may explain the increase in heart disease in post-menopausal women. Consequently, it may be that post-menopausal women should increase their intake of ACE nutrients. Pre-menopausal women may also be protected against heart disease by their hormones.

Supplements and pregnancy

Vitamin A

The advice for women who are pregnant (or who might become pregnant) is not to eat liver or take vitamin A supplements. There have been cases of birth defects in women who took supplements, and one in a woman who ate liver every day. A single 90g/3½ oz portion of liver could now contain 4–12 times the safe amount because of what's going on down on the farm. Food manufacturers are adding vitamin A to animal feeds – and animals are also fed on the offal of other animals, which is high in vitamin A because that is where the body stores this fat-soluble vitamin. The government has asked manufacturers to limit the amount of vitamin A they put in animal feeds and research is going on into how much can safely be added. Meanwhile, the advice not to eat liver, first issued in 1990, is still in force. Foods rich in beta carotene, the non-toxic version of vitamin A, that pregnant women can eat include many green leafy vegetables, watercress, mushrooms, bananas and oranges.

Folic acid

To help prevent the risk of a child being born with spina bifida or other neural tube defect (NTD), all women planning a pregnancy should increase their intake of folic acid by eating more folate-rich foods or by taking a folic acid supplement (400mcg (0.4g) a day) from the time they try to conceive until the twelfth week of pregnancy. This advice comes from the Department of Health. Women who have had an NTD baby are advised to take a supplement of 4 mg a day for the same period. In general, women of reproductive age are advised to treble their intake from 200 mcg to 600 mcg a day.

Foods rich in folic acid include fortified breakfast cereals and wholemeal bread, leafy green vegetables and oranges.

Are you going to take the tablets ?

You have a choice between three different paths to take:

1. Don't take any ACE supplements, but eat plenty of foods rich in ACE nutrients, using *The Ultimate ACE Diet* as your guide. Start with the recipe section (page 105) and build in lots of other delicious foods rich in ACE nutrients (listed in Chapter 4). This doesn't mean a hair-shirt and lentil-soup existence. If your basic diet is good (i.e. supplying the nutrients you need), you can still indulge in some less nutritious foods if you want to. However, even if you do eat well it's not possible to obtain very high doses of ACE nutrients – especially vitamin E.
2. Take an ACE supplement and also eat plenty of foods rich in ACE nutrients, using *The Ultimate ACE Diet* as your guide.
3. Take a standard multi-vitamin and multi-mineral supplement and eat plenty of foods rich in ACE nutrients, using *The Ultimate ACE Diet* as your guide. Try to assess which nutrients are most likely to be lacking in your diet (perhaps because you dislike certain foods) and choose the multi supplement accordingly.

Whatever you decide, it still remains important to make sure that your everyday diet is well balanced according to the principles in this book. Most important of all, ENJOY YOUR FOOD. Pleasure and sharing are things you will never get from popping vitamin pills.

NOTE: IF YOU ARE TAKING ANY MEDICATION CHECK WITH YOUR DOCTOR BEFORE STARTING TO TAKE VITAMIN OR MINERAL SUPPLEMENTS.

CHAPTER 7

The Ultimate ACE Diet Recipes

STARTERS AND LIGHT MEALS
(soups, salads, miscellaneous)

MAIN MEALS
(eggs, vegetarian, fish, meat)

PUDDINGS
(and petits fours)

✻

BAKING
(and breakfast)

✻

Starters and Light Meals

Pistou Soup
Serves 4

900ml/1½pt vegetable stock
225g/8oz new potatoes, scraped
225g/8oz baby carrots, scraped
175g/6oz French beans, trimmed
4 ripe tomatoes, skinned
400g/14oz cannellini (or other white beans)
75g/3oz dry weight pasta shapes
2 tbsp pesto
freshly grated Parmesan cheese, to serve

1. Heat the stock while you prepare the potatoes, carrots and French beans. Add them to the hot stock, cover and simmer for 10 minutes.
2. Add the tomatoes, beans and pasta to the stock and continue to cook, uncovered, for a further 10–12 minutes or until the pasta is cooked but still *al dente*.
3. Remove from the heat. Stir in the pesto and serve with Parmesan cheese.

Nutrient	Units	per portion
Energy	Kcals	332.97
Vitamin **A**	mcg	676.44
Carotene	mcg	3905.75
Vitamin **C**	mg	32.25
Vitamin **E**	mg	0.99
Fibre	g	9.77
Polyunsaturates	g	0.63
Monounsaturates	g	3.93
Saturated fat	g	1.99

Watercress Soup
Serves 4

1 tbsp vegetable oil
1 onion, chopped
2 bunches watercress, washed and trimmed
1 medium potato, diced (about 200g/7oz)
1 litre/1¾ pt vegetable stock
125ml/¼pt fat reduced single cream
salt and pepper

To garnish
sprigs of watercress
freshly grated nutmeg

1. Heat the oil in a large saucepan and sauté the onion until translucent.
2. Add the watercress, potato and stock to the pan. Cover and bring to the boil. Reduce the heat and simmer for 20 minutes.
3. Transfer to a food processor or blender and liquidize. Season with salt and pepper to taste.
4. Sieve for a finer consistency, if preferred, before returning to the pan. Heat through and stir in the cream, reserving 1½ tbsp. Pour into serving bowls, swirl in the reserved cream and top with watercress and a grating of nutmeg.

Nutrient	Units	per portion
Energy	Kcals	132.34
Vitamin **A**	mcg	230.57
Carotene	mcg	1027.13
Vitamin **C**	mg	31.74
Vitamin **E**	mg	0.75
Fibre	g	1.57
Polyunsaturates	g	1.63
Monounsaturates	g	2.93
Saturated fat	g	2.99

Gazpacho
Serves 4

This classic soup is best served immediately after preparing, but if you wish to make it in advance store it in a sealed container in the fridge and whisk again just before serving.

½ medium onion, chopped
450g/1lb ripe tomatoes, skinned and roughly chopped
½ cucumber, chopped
1 red pepper, deseeded and diced
2 cloves garlic, crushed
450ml/¾pt tomato juice
2 tbsp olive oil
1 tbsp white wine vinegar
salt and pepper
few drops Tabasco (optional)
2 tbsp freshly chopped flat-headed parsley

To serve
croûtons
diced peppers
chopped onion
diced cucumber

1. Place all the ingredients except the parsley in a food processor or blender and liquidize. For a smoother result, sieve the soup.
2. Season with salt and pepper and stir in the parsley just before serving with croûtons, peppers, onions and cucumber.

Nutrient	Units	per portion
Energy	Kcals	106.10
Vitamin **A**	mcg	427.50
Carotene	mcg	2577.63
Vitamin **C**	mg	90.51
Vitamin **E**	mg	3.05
Fibre	g	3.07
Polyunsaturates	g	0.82
Monounsaturates	g	4.48
Saturated fat	g	0.83

Lentil and Apricot Soup
Serves 4

1 tbsp vegetable oil
1 onion, diced
1 tsp ground cumin
50g/2oz red lentils
50g/2oz dried apricots
1 large potato (200g/7oz), chopped
1.2 litres/2pt vegetable stock
juice of 1 lemon
salt and pepper
3 tbsp freshly chopped parsley

1. Heat the oil in a large saucepan and sauté the onion and cumin until the onion is translucent.
2. Pick over the lentils, removing any stones. Wash them and place in the saucepan with the apricots, potato, stock and lemon juice.
3. Bring to the boil, cover and simmer for 30 minutes. Remove from the heat and liquidize in a food processor or blender. Return to the heat, season to taste and stir in the parsley just before serving.

Nutrient	Units	per portion
Energy	Kcals	147.65
Vitamin **A**	mcg	66.42
Carotene	mcg	399.67
Vitamin **C**	mg	22.68
Vitamin **E**	mg	0.38
Fibre	g	2.92
Polyunsaturates	g	0.92
Monounsaturates	g	2.18
Saturated fat	g	0.40

Yellow Pepper and Carrot Soup
Serves 4

2 tbsp olive oil
1 onion, chopped
1 clove garlic, crushed
2 yellow peppers, deseeded and chopped
1 large potato, cubed
225g/8oz carrots, sliced
900ml/1½pt vegetable stock or water
pinch of nutmeg
pinch of cayenne pepper
salt and pepper
freshly chopped parsley, to garnish

1. Heat the oil in a pan and sauté the onion, garlic and pepper for about 5 minutes until slightly softened.
2. Add the potato, carrots and stock and simmer for 20 minutes.
3. Transfer to a food processor or blender and liquidize. Pass through a sieve (optional) and return to the pan to heat through.
4. Stir in the parsley and season to taste.

Nutrient	Units	per portion
Energy	Kcals	149.30
Vitamin **A**	mcg	766.48
Carotene	mcg	4598.05
Vitamin **C**	mg	107.79
Vitamin **E**	mg	0.79
Fibre	g	3.89
Polyunsaturates	g	0.87
Monounsaturates	g	4.73
Saturated fat	g	0.82

Red Pepper and Tomato Soup
Serves 4

1 tbsp olive oil
1 onion, chopped
2 red peppers, deseeded and chopped
1 large potato, cubed
4 large carrots, sliced
450g/1lb ripe tomatoes, roughly chopped
300ml/½pt vegetable stock
1 tbsp freshly chopped basil
salt and pepper

1. Heat the oil in a pan and sauté the onion and pepper for about 5 minutes until slightly softened. Add the potato, carrots and tomatoes and continue to cook for a further 10 minutes, stirring to prevent sticking to the pan.
2. Add the stock and simmer for 15 minutes. Transfer to a food processor or blender and liquidize. Pass through a sieve (optional) and return to the pan to heat through.
3. Stir in the basil, season to taste and heat through.

Nutrient	Units	per portion
Energy	Kcals	140.54
Vitamin A	mcg	1875.01
Carotene	mcg	11261.00
Vitamin C	mg	133.40
Vitamin E	mg	1.66
Fibre	g	5.79
Polyunsaturates	g	0.83
Monounsaturates	g	2.66
Saturated fat	g	0.49

Goat's Cheese Crostini with Rocket Salad
Serves 4

1 small wholemeal baguette
100g/4oz crotin or similar goat's cheese
100g/4oz mixed green leaf salad (such as crispy lettuce,
oak leaf, corn salad, endive, chicory)
50g/2oz rocket

Dressing
3 tbsp extra virgin olive oil
1 tsp whole grain mustard
1 tbsp sherry vinegar
freshly ground black pepper

1. Slice the baguette, allowing two slices per person. Thinly slice the cheese and top each slice of bread with the cheese.
2. Toss the mixed salad and rocket together and arrange on four serving plates.
3. Mix the dressing ingredients.
4. Toast the cheese on the baguettes until melted and lightly browned. Place on the salad and offer the dressing separately.

Nutrient	Units	per portion
Energy	Kcals	281.27
Vitamin A	mcg	84.16
Carotene	mcg	175.70
Vitamin C	mg	2.56
Vitamin E	mg	0.73
Fibre	g	3.90
Polyunsaturates	g	1.71
Monounsaturates	g	8.89
Saturated fat	g	4.65

Broad Bean and Pasta Salad
Serves 4

150g/5oz dried wholemeal pasta shells
700g/1½lb broad beans, shelled (about 225g/8oz shelled weight)
125g/4oz bunch spring onions
1 yellow pepper, halved and deseeded
2 tbsp vinaigrette made with lemon juice rather than vinegar
¼ cucumber, finely diced

1. Boil the pasta shells in plenty of water until *al dente* – cooked but still offering some resistance to the teeth. Drain and place in a large serving dish.
2. Boil or steam the beans for 5 minutes. Drain and add to the pasta.
3. Place the pepper under the grill, skin side up, and cook until the skin blisters and chars. Remove from the heat and when cool enough to handle peel off the skin. Cut the flesh into strips and add to the pasta and beans, together with the vinaigrette and cucumber. Toss and serve.

Nutrient	Units	per portion
Energy	Kcals	219.34
Vitamin **A**	mcg	58.20
Carotene	mcg	347.42
Vitamin **C**	mg	78.15
Vitamin **E**	mg	0.52
Fibre	g	7.86
Polyunsaturates	g	1.12
Monounsaturates	g	4.75
Saturated fat	g	0.87

Carrot and Almond Salad
Serves 4

50g/2oz flaked almonds
225g/8oz carrots, peeled and grated
50g/2oz raisins
2 tbsp vinaigrette
2 tbsp freshly chopped parsley

1. Toast the almonds in the grill pan or a dry frying pan (no added oil) until lightly golden. Remove from the heat.
2. Combine with the remaining ingredients and spoon into a serving dish.

Nutrient	Units	per portion
Energy	Kcals	349.27
Vitamin **A**	mcg	1485.55
Carotene	mcg	8912.33
Vitamin **C**	mg	21.50
Vitamin **E**	mg	7.34
Fibre	g	5.66
Polyunsaturates	g	4.00
Monounsaturates	g	18.71
Saturated fat	g	2.69

Flat Bean and Salami Salad
Serves 4

Flat beans are like runner beans. Any kind of green bean can be used in this salad.

350g/12oz new potatoes
225g/8oz flat beans, sliced
50g/2oz salami, cut into strips
75g/3oz spring onions, chopped
25g/1oz freshly chopped parsley
2 tbsp low-fat mayonnaise
freshly chopped parsley, to garnish (optional)

1. Boil, steam or microwave the potatoes until just cooked. Drain and place in a large serving dish.
2. Boil, steam or microwave the beans until lightly cooked. Drain

and run cold water over them to stop the cooking. Place in the serving dish.

3. Stir in the rest of the ingredients and garnish, if liked, with extra parsley.

Nutrient	Units	per portion
Energy	Kcals	163.46
Vitamin A	mcg	90.38
Carotene	mcg	500.81
Vitamin C	mg	43.25
Vitamin E	mg	0.34
Fibre	g	2.67
Polyunsaturates	g	1.80
Monounsaturates	g	4.02
Saturated fat	g	2.62

Salad Tacos
Serves 4

12 taco shells
150g/5oz spring onions
1 green pepper, deseeded and sliced
3 tomatoes, sliced
200g/7oz can red kidney beans, drained
crisp lettuce leaves
75g/3oz mature Cheddar cheese, grated

1. Warm the taco shells under the grill or in a moderate oven, following the instructions on the packet.
2. Mix the salad ingredients together and fill the taco shells. Sprinkle over the grated cheese and serve at once.

Nutrient	Units	per portion
Energy	Kcals	220.05
Vitamin A	mcg	188.03
Carotene	mcg	766.26
Vitamin C	mg	67.86
Vitamin E	mg	1.50
Fibre	g	4.72
Polyunsaturates	g	0.57
Monounsaturates	g	2.73
Saturated fat	g	4.21

Gado Gado
Serves 4

This lightly cooked vegetable salad with peanut sauce is widely enjoyed in South East Asian restaurants in Britain. Here's my approximation.

1 tbsp vegetable oil
1 large onion, sliced
175g/6oz spring greens, finely shredded
2 carrots, cut into matchsticks
125g/4oz mooli, cut into matchsticks
125g/4oz green beans
125g/4oz beansprouts

Quick satay sauce
4 tbsp crunchy peanut butter
1 tbsp sunflower oil with added vitamin E
½ tsp ground coriander
½tsp ground cumin
1tsp brown sugar
1tbsp soya sauce
¼ tsp chilli powder
4 tbsp boiling water
crispy lettuce leaves

To garnish
sliced cucumber
2 free-range eggs, hard-boiled and sliced

1. Heat the oil in a wok or frying pan and stir-fry the onion, spring greens, carrot, mooli and green beans for about 3 minutes.
2. Add the beansprouts and stir in to heat through. Remove from the heat.
3. Place all the satay sauce ingredients in a saucepan and heat through, stirring well until smoothly amalgamated – about 3 minutes.
4. To serve, arrange the vegetables on a bed of crispy lettuce leaves. Garnish with sliced cucumber and egg. Serve the sauce separately.

Nutrient	Units	per portion
Energy	Kcals	330.91
Vitamin **A**	mcg	713.85
Carotene	mcg	3970.74
Vitamin **C**	mg	91.35
Vitamin **E**	mg	6.06
Fibre	g	6.17
Polyunsaturates	g	4.35
Monounsaturates	g	18.65
Saturated fat	g	1.89

Walnut Waldorf Salad
Serves 4

3 crisp eating apples
juice of ½ lemon
4 sticks celery, diced
75g/3oz walnuts, roughly chopped
3 tbsp low-fat mayonnaise
salt and pepper
curly lettuce leaves (such as Tom Thumb)

1. Peel one of the apples and core all of them. Dice the flesh and toss in the lemon juice.
2. Toss the apples, celery and walnuts in the mayonnaise and season to taste.
3. Line a salad bowl or individual dishes with lettuce leaves and spoon the salad mixture into the leaves.

Nutrient	Units	per portion
Energy	Kcals	207.15
Vitamin **A**	mcg	52.80
Carotene	mcg	266.30
Vitamin **C**	mg	10.25
Vitamin **E**	mg	1.49
Fibre	g	3.04
Polyunsaturates	g	10.59
Monounsaturates	g	4.01
Saturated fat	g	1.83

Herring and Beetroot Salad
Serves 4

700g/1½lb new potatoes
¼ onion, finely chopped
2 tbsp freshly chopped chives
2 tbsp low-fat or low-calorie mayonnaise
200g/7oz rollmop herrings
150g/5oz cooked beetroot, diced
2 free-range eggs, hard-boiled and sliced
1 bunch watercress

1. Scrape and boil the new potatoes. Drain and place on one side to cool. Dice the potatoes and mix with the onion, chives and mayonnaise.
2. To assemble the salad, place the herrings in the centre of a large salad dish. Place the beetroot around them in a circle. Add the potato salad in a further concentric circle. Garnish the outer edge with the trimmed watercress and arrange the sliced egg on top.

Nutrient	Units	per portion
Energy	Kcals	384.62
Vitamin A	mcg	197.02
Carotene	mcg	629.62
Vitamin C	mg	44.78
Vitamin E	mg	0.96
Fibre	g	2.93
Polyunsaturates	g	4.69
Monounsaturates	g	10.97
Saturated fat	g	4.09

Broccoli Quiche
Serves 4

Pastry
pinch of cayenne pepper
225g/8oz wholemeal flour
125g/4oz polyunsaturated margarine

Filling
1 tbsp olive oil
1 red onion, sliced
350g/12oz broccoli, cut into florets, stalks trimmed and reserved
2 free-range eggs
200g/7oz natural yogurt
50g/2oz Gruyère cheese, grated
salt and pepper
2 tbsp freshly chopped parsley, to garnish

1. Preheat the oven to 200°C/400°F/Gas Mark 6.
2. Mix the cayenne pepper into the flour. Rub the fat into the flour and add enough water to mix to a soft dough. Roll out on a lightly floured board and line a 20cm/8in flan tin or ring. Prick the base, line with greaseproof paper and weigh it down with baking beans. Bake for 10 minutes. Remove the baking beans and greaseproof paper and place the pastry case on one side.
3. Lower the oven temperature to 190°C/375°F/Gas Mark 4. Heat the oil in a pan and sauté the onion until slightly softened but not brown. Spread the onion across the base of the flan.
4. Blanch the broccoli heads and stalks. Drain and dry on absorbent kitchen paper. Arrange the florets around the edge of the flan and the stalks in the centre.
5. Beat together the eggs, yogurt, cheese and salt and pepper to taste to make a custard.
6. Pour the custard over the broccoli and bake the quiche for about 35 minutes until the top is golden brown and the custard has set. Sprinkle over the parsley before serving.

Nutrient	Units	per portion
Energy	Kcals	579.00
Vitamin **A**	mcg	244.87
Carotene	mcg	885.74
Vitamin **C**	mg	81.63
Vitamin **E**	mg	1.51
Fibre	g	7.69
Polyunsaturates	g	12.05
Monounsaturates	g	16.04
Saturated fat	g	9.17

Stuffed Peppers
Serves 4

4 red or green peppers
150g/5oz bulgur wheat
1tbsp olive oil
150g/5oz chestnut mushrooms, chopped
4 tomatoes, chopped
2 tsp capers
50g/2oz black olives, stoned and chopped
50g/2oz Parmesan cheese (optional)

Nutrient	Units	per portion
Energy	Kcals	315.16
Vitamin **A**	mcg	1101.75
Carotene	mcg	6360.25
Vitamin **C**	mg	224.83
Vitamin **E**	mg	1.71
Fibre	g	4.63
Polyunsaturates	g	1.23
Monounsaturates	g	6.22
Saturated fat	g	3.53

1. Lightly oil a large ovenproof dish and preheat the oven to 190°C/375°F/Gas Mark 5.
2. Place the peppers, still with their stalks on, in a microwave oven on full power for 4 minutes, turning twice during cooking. Alternatively, blanch them in boiling water for about 3 minutes. When cool enough to handle, halve (cutting down through the stalks) and remove the seeds. Place each half in the prepared dish.
3. Cook the bulgur wheat according to the instructions on the packet – some needs only to stand in boiling water, other varieties are cooked for up to 15 minutes. Remove from the pan and drain if all the liquid has not been absorbed.
4. Heat the oil in a pan and sauté the mushrooms. Add the tomatoes and cook to a slightly mushy consistency. Stir in the bulgur, capers and olives. Place a spoonful of the mixture into each shell.

5. Cover the dish and bake for 30 minutes. Remove the cover and sprinkle over the cheese, if using, for the last 10 minutes of cooking. Return the dish to the oven uncovered.

Ratatouille
Serves 4

Serve ratatouille on its own or as a vegetable accompaniment to meat, fish, quiche or other main dish. It is also delicious as a filling for foccacia (small round Italian breads).

3 tbsp olive oil
350g/12oz aubergine, cubed
350g/12oz courgettes, sliced
1 green pepper, deseeded and cut into strips
1 red pepper, deseeded and cut into strips
1 large onion, sliced
225g/8oz tomatoes, chopped
2 tsp herbes de provence
(a mixture of dried herbs – rosemary, sage, thyme,
marjoram, basil, fennel, oregano and mint)

1. Heat the oil in a large heavy-based pan with a well-fitting lid, add the aubergines and courgettes and fry until lightly browned, about 10 minutes, turning frequently.
2. Add the remainder of the vegetables and the herbs and cover the pan to enable them to continue cooking in their own steam without the addition of further fat. They are ready when they are just cooked but not too soft, abut 15–20 minutes.

Nutrient	Units	per portion
Energy	Kcals	145.85
Vitamin **A**	mcg	426.85
Carotene	mcg	2573.67
Vitamin **C**	mg	129.25
Vitamin **E**	mg	1.11
Fibre	g	4.64
Polyunsaturates	g	1.27
Monounsaturates	g	6.91
Saturated fat	g	1.29

Bagna Cauda
Serves 4

This warm dip for crudités (raw vegetables) is excellent for family use or for entertaining. For crudités, choose from: peppers (red/green/yellow), broccoli florets (blanched), carrots, radicchio leaves, chicory (white/red), celery, cucumber, courgettes, radishes, mushrooms. Mop up with crusty wholemeal baguettes.

6 cloves garlic, peeled
150ml/¼ pt skimmed milk
225g/8oz extra virgin olive oil
25g/1oz unsalted butter
100g/4 oz (2 small cans) anchovies
50g/2oz shelled walnuts

1. Simmer the garlic cloves in the milk for about 25 minutes until soft.
2. Place the remaining ingredients in a food processor or blender. Add the garlic and milk and liquidize.
3. Wash out the milk pan and sieve the processed mixture back into the pan to heat through. (If you don't wash the pan the mixture will catch and burn.)
4. Serve immediately, pouring into either a terracotta bagna cauda dish (which has a cavity for a night light beneath to keep the mixture warm at the table), or a warmed dish or bowl.

Nutrient	Units	per portion
Energy	Kcals	767.79
Vitamin **A**	mcg	64.48
Carotene	mcg	29.38
Vitamin **C**	mg	1.59
Vitamin **E**	mg	2.27
Fibre	g	0.74
Polyunsaturates	g	14.41
Monounsaturates	g	52.13
Saturated fat	g	13.64

Pissaladière
Serves 8

This tart originating from the south of France uses for its filling the same topping ingredients as a basic pizza.

1 quantity of shortcrust pastry (see page 118, but use
300g/10oz flour, 130g/4½oz margarine and omit cayenne pepper)
4tbsp olive oil
700g/1½lb onions, chopped
2 cloves garlic, crushed
450g/1lb tomatoes, skinned and chopped
1tbsp tomato purée
1tsp brown sugar
2 tbsp freshly chopped mixed herbs, such as thyme, parsley,
basil and oregano
salt and pepper

To garnish
black olives; 50g/2oz can anchovies

1. Use the pastry mixture to fill a 23cm–25cm/9–10in shortcrust pastry case. Cook following the instructions on page 119.
2. Heat the oil in a pan and cook the onions and garlic for about 20 minutes over a moderate heat.
3. Add the tomatoes, tomato purée and sugar and continue cooking until the mixture is thick and much of the liquid reduced – about 25 minutes. For the last 10 minutes of cooking, stir in the herbs and season to taste.
4. Spread the tomato mixture in the pastry case and arrange the anchovies and olives on top. Reheat, if liked, in a moderate oven for 10 minutes.

Nutrient	Units	per portion
Energy	Kcals	116.76
Vitamin **A**	mcg	86.47
Carotene	mcg	505.37
Vitamin **C**	mg	19.61
Vitamin **E**	mg	0.91
Fibre	g	2.20
Polyunsaturates	g	1.24
Monounsaturates	g	5.22
Saturated fat	g	1.10

Main Meals

Eggs en Piperade
Serves 2

3 tbsp olive oil
1 red pepper, diced
1 green pepper, diced
1 onion, diced
1 clove garlic, crushed
2 large ripe tomatoes, chopped
sea salt and freshly ground black pepper
2 free-range eggs
wholemeal baguette, sliced

1. Preheat the oven to 190°C/375°F/Gas Mark 5.
2. Heat 1 tbsp oil in an ovenproof pan with a lid (a French marmetout is ideal). Sauté the peppers, onion and garlic for about 5 minutes until softened.
3. Add the tomatoes, cover and cook for a further 15 minutes. Season to taste with salt and pepper.
4. Make two wells in the mixture and carefully break one egg into each. Transfer the pan to the oven and bake, uncovered, for 12 minutes to set the eggs.
5. Meanwhile, brush slices of baguette with the remaining olive oil, sprinkle with sea salt and freshly ground pepper and grill or bake on a tray in the oven for 5 minutes.

Nutrient	Units	per portion
Energy	Kcals	540.89
Vitamin A	mcg	741.72
Carotene	mcg	3832.50
Vitamin C	mg	225.13
Vitamin E	mg	2.47
Fibre	g	10.04
Polyunsaturates	g	4.09
Monounsaturates	g	17.49
Saturated fat	g	4.66

Italian Frittata
Serves 4

This is a type of omelette, stuffed full of vegetables and cooked slowly until set, then served flat rather than folded over as for standard omelette. Different fillings are reflected in the Italian names, for example, genovese is with spinach; rognsa contains meat and sausage; alla savoiarda is with ham, potatoes, leeks and cheese; veneta contains anchovies, garlic and tomatoes; and alla siciliana is with cheese, onion and basil, usually served fredda (cold). The filling given here can be made in advance and stored in the fridge until needed.

3 tbsp olive oil
1 onion, chopped
1 clove garlic, crushed
1 red pepper, deseeded and cut into strips
1 medium courgette, sliced
175g/6oz sweetcorn kernels
2 tomatoes, skinned, deseeded and chopped
3 tbsp freshly chopped mixed herbs: basil, parsley,
thyme, tarragon
6 free-range eggs
salt and pepper

Nutrient	Units	per portion
Energy	Kcals	276.69
Vitamin **A**	mcg	535.51
Carotene	mcg	2276.50
Vitamin **C**	mg	83.39
Vitamin **E**	mg	1.52
Fibre	g	2.51
Polyunsaturates	g	2.21
Monounsaturates	g	12.14
Saturated fat	g	3.76

1. Heat 2 tbsp olive oil in a pan and sauté the onion, garlic, pepper and courgette until beginning to soften. Stir in the sweetcorn, tomato and herbs and place on one side.
2. Beat the eggs with salt and pepper and stir in the vegetable mixture.

3. Heat the rest of the oil in a large frying pan and add the egg mixture. Move gently from side to side as it begins to set so that the runny egg in the middle trickles out to the side. Then reduce the heat, cover and cook gently for about 20 minutes until the centre of the frittata is completely set.
4. To serve, invert onto a warmed serving dish and garnish with watercress or other green salad.

Spinach Gnocchi with Tomato Sauce
Serves 4

If you are pressed for time you can use a 300g/10oz tub of ready-made plain tomato pasta sauce rather than making your own.

600ml/1pt skimmed milk
175g/6oz semolina
25g/1oz butter
75g/3oz Parmesan cheese, finely grated
pinch of freshly grated nutmeg
salt and pepper
2 free-range eggs
175g/6oz frozen spinach, thawed and squeezed dry
25g/1oz pine kernels

Tomato sauce
1tbsp olive oil
1 medium onion, chopped
1 clove garlic, crushed
400g/14oz can tomatoes
1 tbsp tomato purée
1 tbsp freshly chopped herbs, e.g. parsley, basil, thyme
freshly ground black pepper

1. To make the tomato sauce, heat the oil in a pan. Add the onion and garlic and cook until translucent. Stir in the remaining ingredients, cover and cook for 20 minutes.
2. Preheat the oven to 190°C/375°F/Gas Mark 5 and lightly oil a 23cm/9in diameter ovenproof dish.
3. Heat the milk in a large saucepan and when on the point of boiling slowly pour in the semolina, stirring until smooth and thick. Continue cooking and stirring for about 2 minutes.

4. Remove from the heat and beat in the butter, cheese, nutmeg and salt and pepper to taste.
5. Leave to cool slightly, then beat in the eggs and spinach.
6. Using two large spoons, form the mixture into balls of about 5cm/2in diameter. Place in the base of the prepared dish. Pour the tomato sauce over the gnocchi, sprinkle on the pine kernels and bake for about 25 minutes.

Nutrient	Units	per portion
Energy	Kcals	463.05
Vitamin **A**	mcg	438.23
Carotene	mcg	1613.44
Vitamin **C**	mg	12.88
Vitamin **E**	mg	1.30
Fibre	g	1.96
Polyunsaturates	g	2.94
Monounsaturates	g	9.25
Saturated fat	g	8.72

Vegetable Risotto
Serves 4

Risotto should be creamy and moist, unlike pilaff and paellas which are drier. You can also stir a risotto during cooking, unlike paellas in particular.

20g/¾oz dried mushrooms such as porcini, morelles, cepes,
champignon or 125g/4oz fresh mushrooms
2 tbsp olive oil
2 cloves garlic, crushed
1 large onion, chopped
1 red pepper, diced
1 green pepper, sliced
3 sticks celery, chopped
225g/8oz risotto (arborio) rice
pinch of saffron strands, or ¼ tsp turmeric
300ml/½pt vegetable stock
1 tbsp freshly chopped basil

1. Soak the dried mushrooms according to the instructions on the packet (usually a minimum of 15 minutes in boiling water).

2. Heat the oil in a large, heavy based saucepan and sauté the garlic, onion, peppers and celery until they soften (about 5 minutes), stirring from time to time.
3. Stir in the rice and cook for a further 5 minutes, stirring to prevent sticking. Add the saffron or turmeric, pour on the stock and the mushrooms, including their soaking water, and bring to simmering point. Simmer for about 20 minutes, or until the rice is cooked. Top up with stock during cooking, if necessary.

Nutrient	Units	per portion
Energy	Kcals	331.26
Vitamin **A**	mcg	276.77
Carotene	mcg	1661.37
Vitamin **C**	mg	103.83
Vitamin **E**	mg	0.70
Fibre	g	2.66
Polyunsaturates	g	1.00
Monounsaturates	g	4.73
Saturated fat	g	0.97

Aubergine and Tomato Pasta Sauce
Serves 4

3 tbsp olive oil
225g/8oz onions, chopped
2 cloves garlic, crushed
450g/1lb tomatoes, skinned and chopped
1 tbsp freshly chopped basil
salt and pepper
1 large aubergine
1 tbsp tomato purée

1. Heat 2 tbsp olive oil in a pan and sauté the onions and garlic for about 10 minutes over a moderate heat.
2. Add the tomatoes and continue cooking until the mixture is thick and much of the liquid is reduced – about 25 minutes. For the last 10 minutes of cooking stir in the basil and season to taste.
3. While the sauce is cooking pierce the aubergine and cook on full power in a microwave oven for 3 minutes, turning once. Alternatively, bake in a preheated moderate oven for 40 minutes.

4. Carefully cube the cooked aubergine, using a knife and fork if too hot to handle. Place in a pan with the remaining olive oil and the tomato purée and cook quickly for 5 minutes. Stir in the tomato sauce and use at once with cooked pasta (you will need about 75g/3oz fresh pasta or 50g/2oz dry pasta per person).

Nutrient	Units	per portion
Energy	Kcals	135.86
Vitamin **A**	mcg	155.08
Carotene	mcg	939.38
Vitamin **C**	mg	28.50
Vitamin **E**	mg	1.33
Fibre	g	4.08
Polyunsaturates	g	1.17
Monounsaturates	g	6.73
Saturated fat	g	1.22

Spinach and Tomato Flan
Serves 6

300g/10oz puff pastry (half a standard pack of 568g/1¼lb)
400g/14oz fresh spinach
¼ tsp ground nutmeg
25g/1oz unsalted butter
freshly ground black pepper
2 tbsp pesto or black olive pâté
black olives, to garnish
700g/1½lb ripe tomatoes, skinned, sliced and roughly deseeded

1. Preheat the oven to 200°C/400°F/Gas Mark 6. Lightly oil a 20cm/8in flan tin.
2. Roll out the pastry and line the tin. Pierce the pastry on the base of the flan with a fork. Line the pastry with greaseproof paper and fill the case with baking beans. Bake blind for 12 minutes, then remove the paper and beans and return to the oven for 5 minutes to dry out and crisp the base.
3. Wash the spinach and place in a saucepan with the nutmeg and butter. Cover and cook for about 5–6 minutes, stirring occasionally, until the spinach is cooked. Transfer to a food processor or blender and blend to a purée. Season to taste with pepper.

4. To assemble the tart, spread the pesto or olive pâté over the base of the tart. Top with the spinach, levelling the top. Arrange the sliced tomatoes over the top and garnish with the olives. Return to the oven for 15 minutes.

Nutrient	Units	per portion
Energy	Kcals	265.80
Vitamin A	mcg	561.01
Carotene	mcg	3191.73
Vitamin C	mg	38.58
Vitamin E	mg	1.75
Fibre	g	2.89
Polyunsaturates	g	0.65
Monounsaturates	g	13.98
Saturated fat	g	2.43

Courgette Bake
Serves 4

700g/1½lb courgettes
225g/8oz tomatoes, sliced
1 green pepper, deseeded and cut into strips
salt and pepper
3 tbsp olive oil
50g/2oz fresh wholemeal breadcrumbs
75g/3oz Parmesan cheese, grated

1. Preheat the oven to 190°C/375°F/Gas Mark 5 and lightly oil a 23cm/9in ovenproof dish.
2. Grate one large courgette into the base of the dish. Top with the tomatoes and green pepper. Season to taste.

Nutrient	Units	per portion
Energy	Kcals	235.86
Vitamin A	mcg	337.61
Carotene	mcg	1662.37
Vitamin C	mg	102.94
Vitamin E	mg	0.97
Fibre	g	3.70
Polyunsaturates	g	1.67
Monounsaturates	g	8.74
Saturated fat	g	5.33

3. Slice the remaining courgettes and arrange the slices in concentric circles on top of the vegetables in the dish. Drizzle over the olive oil and season to taste.
4. Mix the breadcrumbs and Parmesan cheese and place in a layer on top of the dish. Bake for 35 minutes, covering the top of the dish towards the end of cooking to prevent it over-browning.

Pumpkin Curry
Serves 4

2 tbsp oil
2 onions, diced
2 green chillies, finely chopped
2 cloves garlic, crushed
1 tsp ground cumin
1 tsp ground coriander
450g/1lb pumpkin, peeled, seeded and cubed
400g/14oz can tomatoes
450ml/¾pt vegetable stock
400g/14oz can borlotti beans
2tbsp freshly chopped coriander leaves

1. Heat the olive oil in a pan and sauté the onions, chillies, garlic and spices for about 5 minutes, stirring well.
2. Add the pumpkin and cook for a further 5 minutes. Stir in the tomatoes and stock and cover the pan. Simmer for 15 minutes.
3. Stir in the borlotti beans and cook for a further 10 minutes with the lid off the pan to reduce the stock slightly. Stir in the coriander leaves. Serve with brown rice and a green vegetable.

Nutrient	Units	per portion
Energy	Kcals	151.10
Vitamin **A**	mcg	144.98
Carotene	mcg	870.04
Vitamin **C**	mg	39.58
Vitamin **E**	mg	2.11
Fibre	g	2.60
Polyunsaturates	g	1.65
Monounsaturates	g	4.70
Saturated fat	g	0.65

Singapore Noodles
Serves 4

175g/6oz (or ⅔ pack) Sharwoods medium egg noodles
2 tbsp vegetable oil
1 onion, chopped
2 green chillies, finely chopped
1 clove garlic, crushed
1 green pepper, diced
1 large carrot, sliced
4 spring onions, chopped

Sauce
3 tbsp dark soya sauce
1 tbsp red wine vinegar
2 tsp demerara sugar
juice of 1 orange

1. Place the noodles in a large pan of boiling water and remove from the heat immediately. Leave for 6 minutes, then drain.
2. Place all the sauce ingredients in a saucepan and stir over a moderate heat until the sugar is dissolved. Alternatively, place in a microwave-proof jug and cook in the microwave on full power for 2 minutes.
3. Heat the oil in a wok or frying pan and stir-fry the onion, chillies, garlic, pepper and carrot until just softening. Stir in the spring onions.
4. Add the sauce to the vegetables and heat through. Remove from the heat and stir in the prepared noodles.

Nutrient	Units	per portion
Energy	Kcals	268.36
Vitamin A	mcg	339.04
Carotene	mcg	1935.53
Vitamin C	mg	61.85
Vitamin E	mg	0.88
Fibre	g	1.84
Polyunsaturates	g	5.24
Monounsaturates	g	3.23
Saturated fat	g	1.00

Vegetable Chop Suey
Serves 4

2 tbsp vegetable oil
1 onion, chopped
1 green pepper, sliced
1 large carrot, cut into matchsticks
125g/4oz mushrooms
125g/4oz beansprouts
1 can Sharwoods stir-fry chop suey sauce

1. Heat the oil in a wok or frying pan and stir-fry the onion, pepper, carrot and mushrooms for 5 minutes.
2. Add the beansprouts and stir in the chop suey sauce. Heat through.

Nutrient	Units	per portion
Energy	Kcals	103.57
Vitamin **A**	mcg	302.06
Carotene	mcg	1812.63
Vitamin **C**	mg	48.57
Vitamin **E**	mg	0.94
Fibre	g	2.13
Polyunsaturates	g	3.25
Monounsaturates	g	1.94
Saturated fat	g	0.81

Provençale Pie
Serves 8

1 tbsp olive oil
½ red pepper, deseeded and cut into strips
1 large onion, diced
1 clove garlic, crushed
125g/4oz green beans, blanched and sliced
1 tbsp freshly chopped thyme
8 sheets filo pastry, thawed if frozen
(each sheet measuring 30 x 15cm/12 x 6in)
40g/1½oz unsalted butter, melted
1tbsp pesto sauce or black olive pâté
400g/14oz can artichoke hearts, drained
125g/4oz feta cheese, crumbled
50g/2oz black olives, pitted and chopped

1. Preheat the oven to 200°C/400°F/Gas Mark 6. Lightly oil a 20cm/8in loose-bottomed cake tin or flan ring set on a baking sheet.
2. Heat the oil in a pan and sauté the pepper, onion, garlic and beans with the thyme until soft, about 8 minutes. Remove from the heat and set on one side.
3. To prepare the pastry case, line the tin with 6 sheets of pastry, brushing with a little butter between each sheet. Ensure that the base and sides are well covered and allow excess pastry to overhang the sides of the tin.
4. To assemble the pie, spread the base with the pesto or olive pâté. Pack in the other ingredients, ensuring an even mix of ingredients throughout the pie.

Nutrient	Units	per portion
Energy	Kcals	126.82
Vitamin A	mcg	129.77
Carotene	mcg	471.04
Vitamin C	mg	17.43
Vitamin E	mg	0.29
Fibre	g	2.06
Polyunsaturates	g	0.38
Monounsaturates	g	3.41
Saturated fat	g	3.68

5. Top the pie with the remaining 2 pastry sheets, brushing each with butter and tucking in the overhanging ends from the base of the pie. Brush the top with the remaining butter, cover with a piece of foil and bake for 30 minutes, removing the foil for the last 15 minutes so that the pastry turns golden brown.

Caribbean Vegetables and Corn Bread
Serves 4

2 tbsp corn oil
1 red pepper, chopped
1 green pepper, chopped
2 chilli peppers (preferably Scotch bonnets), diced
1 medium sweet potato, cubed
1 plantain, peeled and sliced
50g/2oz okra, topped, tailed and sliced
2 large tomatoes, roughly chopped
2 cloves garlic, crushed
2.5cm/1in piece root ginger, peeled and grated
pinch of cayenne pepper
300ml/½pt vegetable stock

Corn Bread
1 free-range egg
120ml/4 fl oz skimmed milk
150g/5oz cornmeal (maize flour)
75g/3oz unbleached or wholemeal flour
2tsp baking powder
sea salt

1. Heat the oil in a large pan, add all the other ingredients except the stock and sauté for about 15 minutes, stirring frequently to prevent sticking. Keep the pan covered between stirring to seal in the moisture.
2. Add the stock, cover and cook for a further 10–15 minutes.
3. To make the corn bread, preheat the oven to 200°C/400°F/Gas Mark 6.
4. Lightly beat the egg with the milk.
5. Sift the flours and baking powder into a mixing bowl. Make a well in the centre and gradually work in the liquid.

6. Place in a lightly oiled 450g/1lb bread tin. Sprinkle the top with salt and bake for 30 minutes, or until golden brown and an inserted skewer comes out clean.
7. Serve the vegetables with slices of corn bread to mop up the delicious juices.

Nutrient	Units	per portion
Energy	Kcals	166.66
Vitamin A	mcg	530.67
Carotene	mcg	3192.55
Vitamin C	mg	130.01
Vitamin E	mg	2.05
Fibre	g	3.65
Polyunsaturates	g	3.23
Monounsaturates	g	2.41
Saturated fat	g	0.84

Aubergine Cannelloni
Serves 4

2 aubergines
225g/8oz ricotta cheese
1 tbsp freshly chopped basil
50g/2oz Parmesan cheese, grated

Spicy Tomato Sauce
2 tbsp olive oil
1 onion, diced
1 clove garlic, crushed
1 chilli pepper, deseeded and diced
1 tbsp fresh thyme
6 halves sun-dried tomatoes
400g/14oz can tomatoes

1. Preheat the oven to 180°C/350°F/Gas Mark 4. Lightly oil a large ovenproof dish.
2. To prepare the 'cannelloni', trim the aubergines and cut them into 1cm/½in slices lengthways. Place in a microwave-proof dish and cover. Cook on full power for 2–3 minutes until the slices are soft and partially cooked. (Alternatively, brush the slices with oil and bake for 30 minutes in a moderate oven on a baking sheet.) Allow to cool.

136

3. While the aubergine slices are cooling, make the sauce. Heat the oil in a pan and sauté the onion, garlic, chilli, thyme and sun-dried tomatoes for about 10 minutes. Add the canned tomatoes and cook for 15 minutes. Place the sauce in a food processor or blender and liquidize to a smooth purée.
4. To assemble, mix the ricotta cheese and basil and spread each slice of aubergine with a spoonful. Roll up to make the cannelloni and place in the prepared dish. Pour the tomato sauce over the cannelloni. Sprinkle the Parmesan cheese over the top and bake for 20 minutes.

Nutrient	Units	per portion
Energy	Kcals	270.38
Vitamin **A**	mcg	357.66
Carotene	mcg	1263.75
Vitamin **C**	mg	46.09
Vitamin **E**	mg	1.73
Fibre	g	4.12
Polyunsaturates	g	1.13
Monounsaturates	g	14.16
Saturated fat	g	3.70

Stir-Fried Green Vegetables
Serves 4

Even people who don't usually like to eat up their greens can be partial to Chinese food, and a stir-fry is an excellent way of enjoying lightly cooked green vegetables. Spring greens or green cabbage can also be successfully stir fried – add a few sesame seeds to enhance their flavour.

2 tbsp vegetable oil
2 cloves garlic, crushed
2.5cm/1in piece root ginger, peeled and grated
1 green pepper, sliced
1 large leek, sliced
2 courgettes, cut into strips
175g/6oz broccoli florets
125g/4oz mangetout, topped and tailed
4 spring onions, chopped

Nutrient	Units	per portion
Energy	Kcals	100.78
Vitamin A	mcg	192.78
Carotene	mcg	1153.94
Vitamin C	mg	116.54
Vitamin E	mg	1.36
Fibre	g	3.88
Polyunsaturates	g	3.17
Monounsaturates	g	2.58
Saturated fat	g	0.78

1. Heat the oil in a wok or frying pan and stir-fry the garlic, ginger and green pepper for about 3 minutes.
2. Add the leek, courgette, broccoli florets and mangetout and continue cooking for a further 4 minutes.
3. Add the spring onions and heat through. Serve immediately with soya sauce.

Broccoli and Ham Pasta
Serves 4

2 corn cobs
25g/1oz butter
salt and pepper
300g/10oz broccoli, cut into florets
225g/8oz fresh tagliatelle
175g/6oz Virginia ham
2 tbsp freshly chopped parsley

Nutrient	Units	per portion
Energy	Kcals	371.39
Vitamin A	mcg	170.19
Carotene	mcg	716.12
Vitamin C	mg	79.75
Vitamin E	mg	0.97
Fibre	g	4.73
Polyunsaturates	g	1.11
Monounsaturates	g	4.80
Saturated fat	g	4.17

1. Boil or microwave the corn until just cooked. Cut the kernels from the cobs and place in a large serving dish. Toss in the butter and season well.
2. Boil, steam or microwave the broccoli until just cooked but still firm. Drain and add to the corn.
3. Cook the pasta according to the instructions on the packet, usually in plenty of lightly salted water for about 3-4 minutes. Drain and add to the serving dish.
4. While the pasta is cooking shred the ham and add to the dish, along with the parsley. Toss all the ingredients well and serve immediately.

Poussin Provençale
Serves 4

2 poussins
4 tbsp olive oil
1½ red pepper, deseeded and cut into strips
1½ green pepper, deseeded and cut into strips
2 large courgettes, sliced
2 tsp herbes de provence
(a mixture of dried herbs – rosemary, sage, thyme,
marjoram, basil, fennel, oregano and mint)
salt and pepper

1. Preheat the oven to 190°C/375°F/Gas Mark 5.
2. To prepare the poussins, place them breast side down on a chopping board. Using poultry shears (or strong kitchen scissors) cut along each side of the backbones and discard. Trim off flaps of skin and wing tips. Turn the birds upside down and snip the wishbones, then push down on the breasts to flatten them. Make a small cut in the skin between the leg and breastbone and, with the legs turned in, neatly tuck in the leg knuckles. The birds are now ready for grilling or frying.
3. Place half the oil in an ovenproof dish (with a lid) that is large enough to accommodate two flattened poussins.
4. Lightly brown the poussins in the dish over a moderate heat. Remove and place on one side.

Nutrient	Units	per portion
Energy	Kcals	479.87
Vitamin A	mcg	435.35
Carotene	mcg	2616.51
Vitamin C	mg	154.13
Vitamin E	mg	0.88
Fibre	g	2.14
Polyunsaturates	g	5.79
Monounsaturates	g	22.84
Saturated fat	g	9.50

5. Fry the vegetables briskly in the dish to brown them lightly. Lay the poussins on top and sprinkle over the remaining oil, herbs and salt and pepper.
6. Cover and bake for 40 minutes. Remove the lid for the final 15 minutes. Serve with new potatoes, boiled

Gammon Steaks with Curried Fruit
Serves 4

4 gammon steaks
1 medium mango, peeled and cubed
2 peaches, peeled and sliced
1 banana, sliced
3 tbsp curried fruit chutney

1. Grill the gammon steaks for about 8 minutes, turning once or twice.
2. Prepare the fruit and mix it well with the chutney. Serve with the gammon and brown rice.

Nutrient	Units	per portion
Energy	Kcals	445.97
Vitamin A	mcg	382.29
Carotene	mcg	2292.66
Vitamin C	mg	68.45
Vitamin E	mg	0.91
Fibre	g	4.69
Polyunsaturates	g	2.07
Monounsaturates	g	4.13
Saturated fat	g	3.10

Stuffed Aubergines
Serves 2 as main course, 4 as starter

2 aubergines
175g/6oz lean lamb, minced
1tsp ground cumin
salt and pepper
175g/6oz cold cooked rice
(or left-over Vegetable Risotto, page 127)
2 tbsp olive oil
50g/2oz Parmesan cheese, grated

1. Preheat the oven to 190°C/375°F/Gas Mark 5.
2. Pierce the aubergines and microwave on full power for 3 minutes, turning once during cooking. Remove and allow to cool slightly. Alternatively, pierce and place directly on the middle shelf of the preheated oven for 45 minutes.
3. Brown the lamb in a pan (without adding fat), together with the cumin and salt and pepper to taste. Cook for about 5 minutes. Stir in the rice and heat through.
4. Halve the aubergines and scoop out the central flesh, leaving a shell to be filled with the meat mixture.
5. Spoon the oil into an ovenproof dish big enough to take the 4 aubergine halves side by side. Place the filled aubergine halves in the dish. Spoon over any remaining meat mixture.
6. Bake for 10 minutes, then remove from the oven and sprinkle the cheese over the top. Return to the oven for a further 15 minutes.

Nutrient	Units	per portion
Energy	Kcals	517.52
Vitamin **A**	mcg	140.00
Carotene	mcg	315.00
Vitamin **C**	mg	15.00
Vitamin **E**	mg	0.56
Fibre	g	7.68
Polyunsaturates	g	1.98
Monounsaturates	g	16.19
Saturated fat	g	10.45

Chicken Slice
Serves 4

450g/1lb fresh spinach
8 sheets filo pastry, thawed if frozen
(each sheet measuring 30 x 15cm/12 x 6in)
15g/½oz butter, melted
225g/8oz ratatouille (page 121)
2 free-range chicken breasts, skinned and boned, cut into strips
2 tsp capers (optional)

1. Preheat the oven to 200°C/400°F/Gas Mark 6.
2. Wash the spinach leaves and place in a saucepan without additional water. Put on the lid and cook, turning once or twice, for about 5 minutes. Remove from the heat and drain, squeezing out excess water.
3. Lightly oil a Swiss roll tin measuring 25cm x 15cm/10 x 6in and place 4 layers of filo pastry, buttering between each layer, in the base.
4. Spread the ratatouille over the pastry. Top with the chicken. Sprinkle over the capers, if using, and add the spinach.
5. Top with 2 of the remaining layers of filo, buttering between them. Crumble the other 2 layers on top and brush with the remaining butter.
6. Bake, covered with foil, for 15 minutes. Remove the foil and return to the oven for a further 10 minutes until the pastry is golden.

Nutrient	Units	per portion
Energy	Kcals	237.59
Vitamin A	mcg	706.67
Carotene	mcg	4094.39
Vitamin C	mg	37.00
Vitamin E	mg	1.47
Fibre	g	2.48
Polyunsaturates	g	1.63
Monounsaturates	g	5.23
Saturated fat	g	3.14

Pork and Rice
Serves 4

2 tbsp olive oil
350g/12oz lean pork, cubed
225g/8oz chestnut mushrooms, sliced
1 onion, diced
1tsp ground coriander
pinch of saffron strands
125g/4oz brown basmati rice
600ml/1pt vegetable stock
4 large ripe tomatoes, chopped

1. Heat the oil in a large, heavy-based saucepan with a well-fitting lid and lightly fry the pork, mushrooms and onion with the spices.
2. Add the rice and stir in well. Continue to cook for about 5 minutes, stirring well. Add the stock and tomatoes and bring to the boil. Lower the heat and simmer, covered, for 25 minutes. Remove the lid and continue cooking for another 10 minutes.

Nutrient	Units	per portion
Energy	Kcals	305.32
Vitamin **A**	mcg	167.71
Carotene	mcg	1021.28
Vitamin **C**	mg	27.19
Vitamin **E**	mg	1.47
Fibre	g	2.91
Polyunsaturates	g	2.51
Monounsaturates	g	7.15
Saturated fat	g	3.17

Meatballs with Red Pepper Sauce
Serves 4

450g/1lb lean lamb, minced
1 large onion, chopped
2 cloves garlic, crushed
20g /¾oz fresh coriander, chopped
75g/3oz pine kernels, lightly toasted
salt and pepper

For the sauce
1tbsp corn oil
1 red pepper, deseeded and chopped
1 onion, chopped
4 ripe tomatoes, skinned and chopped
salt and pepper

1. Place all the meatball ingredients except the pine kernels in a food processor or blender and purée to a smooth mixture. Stir in the pine kernels. Form the mixture into balls in the palms of your hands and place on one side, or in the fridge, until needed.
2. To make the sauce, heat the oil in a pan and sweat the pepper and onion until softened. Add the tomatoes, cover and cook for about 15 minutes until soft. Transfer to a food processor or liquidizer and blend to a purée. Return to the pan, season to taste and thin to the desired consistency with water.
3. Lightly fry or grill the meatballs until golden brown, turning to cook evenly. Remove from the pan and drain on absorbent kitchen paper. Place in a serving dish and pour the red pepper sauce over them.

Nutrient	Units	per portion
Energy	Kcals	442.10
Vitamin A	mcg	383.72
Carotene	mcg	2311.13
Vitamin C	mg	84.40
Vitamin E	mg	3.42
Fibre	g	2.97
Polyunsaturates	g	11.09
Monounsaturates	g	13.25
Saturated fat	g	7.28

Spicy Meat Peppers
Serves 4

4 mixed peppers (yellow, red, green)
2 tbsp sunflower oil with added vitamin E
225g/8oz onion, chopped
1 clove garlic, crushed
1 tbsp chopped fresh mint
¼ tsp ground cinnamon
¼ tsp ground paprika
450g/1lb lean minced leg of lamb
175g/6oz tomatoes, skinned and chopped
175g/6oz long-grain brown rice
100g/4oz raisins
6 tbsp stock
50g/2oz walnut pieces, chopped
600ml/1pt water

1. Preheat the oven to 190°C/375°F/Gas Mark 5.
2. Cut a thin slice from the stalk end of each pepper and reserve. Remove the seeds. Place side by side in a shallow ovenproof dish.
3. Heat the oil in a saucepan and sauté the onion with the garlic, mint, cinnamon and parika for 3–4 minutes. Add the minced lamb and cook, stirring, over a high heat until lightly browned. Carefully pour off the excess fat. Stir in the remaining ingredients and bring to simmering point. Simmer for 20 minutes until the rice is half-cooked and the liquids almost absorbed.
4. Fill the peppers with the meat and rice mixture. Replace the reserved tops.
5. Cover the dish loosely with foil and bake for about 40 minutes.

Nutrient	Units	per portion
Energy	Kcals	610.42
Vitamin **A**	mcg	423.18
Carotene	mcg	2543.14
Vitamin **C**	mg	206.49
Vitamin **E**	mg	6.77
Fibre	g	5.50
Polyunsaturates	g	10.00
Monounsaturates	g	9.27
Saturated fat	g	6.78

Chicken and Chorizo Paella
Serves 4

2 tbsp olive oil
4 chicken thighs
50g/2oz chorizo (spicy Spanish sausage)
1 large onion, chopped
2 cloves garlic, crushed
1 red pepper, deseeded and chopped
1 green pepper, deseeded and chopped
125g/4oz green beans, trimmed and sliced
12 uncooked king prawns in their shells
225g/8oz paella (short grain or arborio) rice
125g/4oz peas
900 ml/1½pt chicken stock
pinch of saffron strands

To garnish
2 tsp freshly chopped parsley
lemon wedges

Nutrient	Units	per portion
Energy	Kcals	473.82
Vitamin A	mcg	288.64
Carotene	mcg	1701.88
Vitamin C	mg	109.05
Vitamin E	mg	0.77
Fibre	g	3.92
Polyunsaturates	g	1.60
Monounsaturates	g	9.12
Saturated fat	g	3.70

1. Heat the oil in a paella pan or large frying pan or saucepan. Cook the chicken pieces until golden. Lift out and place on one side.
2. Add the sausage, onion, garlic, peppers and beans to the pan and cook, stirring, over a moderate heat for about 10 minutes.
3. Add the prawns and cook just until they turn pink.
4. Return the chicken to the pan. Add the rice and peas and stir well. Pour in the stock and saffron and cook over a very low heat until the rice is tender and the liquid absorbed – about

146

30–40 minutes. Unlike risotto, paella is not stirred once the stock is added, though if you are not using a paella pan you might like to stir the pan once just to bring the rice from the edges into the centre to aid even cooking.

Middle Eastern Lamb
Serves 4

1 tbsp olive oil
450g/1lb lean lamb, cubed
1 onion, chopped
1 tsp ground coriander
1 tsp ground cumin
½ tsp ground cinnamon
½ tsp ground ginger
225g/8oz dried apricots, chopped
50g/2oz pine kernels
50g/2oz currants
350g/12oz long-grain brown rice
1 litre/1¾pt vegetable stock or water
salt and pepper
2 tbsp freshly chopped flat-headed parsley, plus extra to garnish

1. Heat the oil in a large heavy-based pan and brown the lamb. Remove from the pan. Add the onion and spices to the pan and sauté for 5 minutes. Add the apricots, pine kernels and currants and continue cooking, stirring to prevent sticking, for a further 5 minutes.
2. Add the lamb and rice and continue cooking, stirring to prevent sticking, for a further 5 minutes.

Nutrient	Units	per portion
Energy	Kcals	746.73
Vitamin **A**	mcg	121.40
Carotene	mcg	736.19
Vitamin **C**	mg	15.38
Vitamin **E**	mg	2.81
Fibre	g	7.04
Polyunsaturates	g	5.68
Monounsaturates	g	11.72
Saturated fat	g	6.98

3. Add half the stock or water and stir well. Cover and leave to simmer for about 30 minutes, stirring occasionally. Add the remaining stock and simmer for a further 30 minutes.
4. When the rice is cooked and the liquid absorbed (but not too dry) season to taste and stir in the parsley. Serve garnished with extra parsley.

Spinach and Ham Roulade
Serves 8

Roulade
25g/1oz butter
25g/1oz flour
150ml¼pt skimmed milk
3 free-range eggs, separated
25g/1oz Gruyère cheese, grated
25g/1oz Parmesan cheese, grated
450g/1lb fresh spinach, cooked, squeezed dry and finely chopped, or
225g/8oz frozen spinach, squeezed dry and finely chopped
freshly ground black pepper
freshly grated nutmeg

Filling
225g/8oz low-fat curd cheese
6 halves of sun-dried tomatoes, chopped
75g/3oz dry-cured ham (e.g. Parma, Serrano), finely shredded

1. Preheat the oven to 180°C/350°F/Gas Mark 4. Lightly oil a Swiss roll tin measuring 25 x 15cm/10 x 6in and line with greaseproof paper.
2. Melt the butter and flour in a saucepan, stirring over a moderate heat to make a roux. Gradually stir in the milk to make a thick paste. Remove from the heat and cool slightly.
3. Beat in the egg yolks and cheese and stir in the spinach. Season with pepper and nutmeg to taste.
4. Whisk the egg whites until stiff and fold into the spinach mixture. Spread the mixture into the prepared tin and bake for 15 minutes, until set and springy to the touch.
5. Remove from the oven and invert onto a clean surface. Peel off the paper and trim the edges. Allow to cool slightly.

Nutrient	Units	per portion
Energy	Kcals	110.95
Vitamin **A**	mcg	421.64
Carotene	mcg	2015.76
Vitamin **C**	mg	14.78
Vitamin **E**	mg	0.78
Fibre	g	1.28
Polyunsaturates	g	0.58
Monounsaturates	g	3.12
Saturated fat	g	3.65

6. Mix together the filling ingredients and spread over the roulade. Roll up and serve with a tomato salad and/or green salad and crusty bread.

Chicken Kebabs
Serves 4

4 x 125g/4oz skinned and boned chicken breasts
juice of 1 lime
1 tbsp clear honey
125g/4oz baby corn
200g/7oz baby courgettes
1 red pepper, deseeded and cut into bite-size pieces
175g/6 oz cherry tomatoes
salt and pepper

Nutrient	Units	per portion
Energy	Kcals	167.99
Vitamin **A**	mcg	379.66
Carotene	mcg	2282.60
Vitamin **C**	mg	96.93
Vitamin **E**	mg	0.58
Fibre	g	2.11
Polyunsaturates	g	0.57
Monounsaturates	g	2.18
Saturated fat	g	1.11

1. Cube the chicken and marinate in the lime juice and honey for at least 2 hours.

2. Boil or microwave the corn, courgettes and pepper until they start to soften.
3. Arrange the chicken, corn, courgettes, pepper and tomatoes on four kebab skewers 30cm/12in in length. Season the kebabs (don't season until just before cooking, otherwise the salt will draw out the moisture from the meat and make the kebabs dry). Heat the grill (or barbecue) and grill under a high heat, basting with the marinade.
4. Serve with a green salad and new potatoes or plain rice.

Chilli Stuffed Cabbage Leaves
Serves 4

12 large green cabbage leaves
125g/4oz bulgur wheat
225g/8oz lean lamb, pork or beef, minced
2 onions, chopped
2 cloves garlic, crushed
2 green chillies, finely chopped
2 ripe tomatoes, chopped
1 tsp ground cumin
salt and pepper
1 tbsp olive oil
400g/14oz can chopped tomatoes

1. Blanch the leaves (plunge in boiling salted water for 2 minutes) and drain, keeping them separate. (This is most easily done by hanging them over a colander.)

Nutrient	Units	per portion
Energy	Kcals	257.21
Vitamin A	mcg	282.42
Carotene	mcg	1702.76
Vitamin C	mg	100.80
Vitamin E	mg	1.30
Fibre	g	5.58
Polyunsaturates	g	1.09
Monounsaturates	g	2.85
Saturated fat	g	2.52

2. Cook the bulgur wheat according to instructions on the packet. (Some needs only to stand in boiling water, other varieties are cooked for up to 15 minutes.) Remove from the pan and leave to cool slightly.
3. Brown the meat with half the onion, half the garlic, the chillies and cumin in a covered pan for about 10 minutes, stirring well from time to time to prevent sticking. Add the 2 ripe tomatoes for the last 5 minutes. Season to taste and remove from the heat. Stir in the bulgur wheat.
4. Place a tablespoonful of meat mixture in each of the leaves, fold over the edges and roll up to encase the filling.
5. Sauté the remaining onion and garlic in a large heavy-based saucepan with a well-fitting lid until softened. Add the canned tomatoes and mix in well. Place the stuffed cabbage leaves in the tomato sauce. Cover and simmer for about 15 minutes.

Chicken Stew with Mango Salad
Serves 4

3 tbsp corn oil
2 onions, diced
2 green chillies, finely chopped
2.5cm/1in piece root ginger, peeled and grated
3 chicken breasts, skinned, boned and cubed
400g/14oz can tomatoes, roughly chopped
2 heaped tbsp crunchy peanut butter
1 aubergine, cubed
125g/4oz okra, topped and tailed
juice of 1 lemon

Mango salad
½ mango, cubed
1 orange, peeled and segmented
1 pink grapefruit, peeled and segmented
crispy lettuce leaves

1. Heat 1 tbsp oil in a pan and sauté the onions, chillies and ginger. Add the chicken and continue cooking gently, stirring well, for about 10 minutes.
2. Stir in the tomatoes and peanut butter and leave to cook over a very low heat while preparing the vegetables.

151

3. Heat the remaining oil in a pan and sauté the aubergine and whole okra until just soft (about 5 minutes). Drain and stir into the chicken stew.
4. Mix well and continue to cook for about 5 minutes, stirring from time to time.
5. Arrange the prepared fruit on the lettuce to make a salad and served with the chicken stew.

Nutrient	Units	per portion
Energy	Kcals	409.21
Vitamin **A**	mcg	333.60
Carotene	mcg	2003.80
Vitamin **C**	mg	91.55
Vitamin **E**	mg	2.68
Fibre	g	7.30
Polyunsaturates	g	6.65
Monounsaturates	g	12.86
Saturated fat	g	2.53

Spicy Prawns and Peppers
Serves 4

2 tbsp vegetable oil
1/4 tsp chilli powder
1cm/1/2in piece root ginger, peeled and grated
1tsp ground black pepper
1 onion, sliced
1 yellow pepper, sliced
1 red pepper, chopped
225g/8oz can bamboo shoots, drained
225g/8oz large shelled cooked prawns
1 tbsp freshly chopped coriander leaves

1. Heat the oil in a wok or frying pan and add the chilli powder, ginger and black pepper. Stir well and add the onion, peppers and bamboo shoots. Stir-fry until just softening, about 2–3 minutes.
2. Add the prawns and cook long enough for them to heat through – about 2–3 minutes. Sprinkle over the coriander and serve.

152

Nutrient	Units	per portion
Energy	Kcals	147.80
Vitamin **A**	mcg	264.10
Carotene	mcg	1584.43
Vitamin **C**	mg	104.00
Vitamin **E**	mg	0.97
Fibre	g	2.19
Polyunsaturates	g	3.21
Monounsaturates	g	2.82
Saturated fat	g	0.91

Thai Stir-Fried Prawns and Vegetables
Serves 4 (with other dishes and/or rice)

A Thai stir-fry contains the typical Thai flavours of chillies, coriander or coconut. Lemon grass and kaffir lime leaves, found in Thai soups and other dishes, are not suitable for adding to stir-fries, although you can add lemon and lime juice instead.

2 tbsp vegetable oil
1 red chilli, finely chopped
1 onion, sliced
125g/4oz mangetout
125g/4oz baby sweetcorn
175g/6oz broccoli florets
125g/4oz beansprouts
175g/6oz large shelled prawns
freshly ground black pepper
1 tbsp freshly chopped coriander leaves

Sauce
50g/2oz creamed coconut
150ml/¼pt boiling water
juice of ½ lime and a little zest
1 stem lemon grass, bruised

1. To prepare the sauce, place the coconut in a pan and dissolve in the boiling water. When creamy stir in the lime juice and zest and add the lemon grass. Gently heat through while stir-frying the vegetables.
2. Heat the oil in a wok or frying pan and stir fry the chilli and onion for 2 minutes.

153

3. Add the mangetout, sweetcorn, and broccoli florets and continue stir-frying until the vegetables are just softening. Stir in the beansprouts, prawns and sauce and heat through.
4. Just before serving, stir in freshly ground black pepper and the coriander leaves.

Nutrient	Units	per portion
Energy	Kcals	217.32
Vitamin **A**	mcg	94.78
Carotene	mcg	570.06
Vitamin **C**	mg	71.21
Vitamin **E**	mg	1.16
Fibre	g	4.62
Polyunsaturates	g	3.31
Monounsaturates	g	3.93
Saturated fat	g	7.53

Grilled Tuna with Red Salsa
Serves 4

1 red pepper
4 x 150g/5oz tuna (or salmon) steaks
4 ripe tomatoes
1 tbsp freshly chopped basil
1 tbsp olive oil
juice of 1 lemon
2 tbsp orange juice
sea salt and freshly ground black pepper
olive oil for grilling

1. Preheat the grill. Halve the pepper and remove the seeds and stalk. Crush lightly to flatten and place under the grill, skin side uppermost, until the skin is black and blistered.
2. When cool enough to handle peel or scrape off the skin and chop the flesh finely.
3. Plunge the tomatoes into boiling water and leave to stand for 3–4 minutes. Drain and place in cold water until cool enough to skin, seed and chop.
4. Mix the peppers and tomatoes with the rest of the ingredients and season to taste. Serve hot or cold with the grilled tuna

Nutrient	Units	per portion
Energy	Kcals	286.01
Vitamin **A**	mcg	362.50
Carotene	mcg	2085.77
Vitamin **C**	mg	72.33
Vitamin **E**	mg	0.89
Fibre	g	1.46
Polyunsaturates	g	4.19
Monounsaturates	g	9.72
Saturated fat	g	4.30

steaks. To heat, either microwave on full power until piping hot (2–3 minutes) or place in a saucepan and stir over a moderate heat for 7 minutes.

5. To grill the tuna steaks, brush lightly with olive oil and season with sea salt and freshly ground black pepper. Place under a preheated grill and cook, turning once, for about 5 minutes on each side (the exact cooking time will depend on the thickness of the steaks).

Salmon Fishcakes with Salsa Verde
Serves 4

Salsa verde is a term that covers a wide variety of green sauces made by blending herbs and oil. The fish cakes can be made with canned salmon (use a 400g/14oz can), but fresh salmon is nicest. Salsa verde is also delicious with pasta and vegetables and grilled or barbecued fish.

350g/12oz floury potatoes
2 tbsp low-fat mayonnaise
350–450g/12oz–1lb salmon (use tailpiece)
1 tbsp freshly chopped parsley
1 tbsp freshly chopped dill
salt and pepper
75g/3oz fresh wholemeal breadcrumbs, toasted
2 tbsp vegetable oil for frying

Salsa verde
4 tbsp freshly chopped flat-headed parsley
1 clove garlic, crushed
1 tbsp capers, chopped
120ml/4fl oz olive oil
2 tbsp lemon juice
salt and pepper

1. Combine all the salsa verde ingredients in a clean screwtop jar and shake well.
2. Boil the potatoes and mash half of them with the mayonnaise. Dice the other half to give the fishcakes some texture.
3. Either poach or microwave the salmon until it just flakes off the bone. To microwave, place in a covered dish or wrap in grease-proof or microwave paper and cook on full power for about 3 minutes (check oven manufacturer's cooking instructions). To poach, place in a saucepan or flameproof dish and add veg-etable stock or court bouillon to about halfway up the sides of the fish steaks. Bring the liquid to simmering point for about 5 minutes. Drain.
4. Skin and bone the fish and flake the flesh with a fork. Mix with the potato, herbs and salt and pepper.
5. Form into fish cakes and roll in the breadcrumbs. Fry lightly and serve with the salsa verde and green vegetables such as broccoli and peas or mangetout.

Nutrient	Units	per portion
Energy	Kcals	582.76
Vitamin **A**	mcg	123.39
Carotene	mcg	630.15
Vitamin **C**	mg	38.69
Vitamin **E**	mg	1.81
Fibre	g	3.22
Polyunsaturates	g	7.67
Monounsaturates	g	28.94
Saturated fat	g	7.59

Puddings

Blackcurrant Summer Fruit Compote
Serves 4

225g/8oz blackcurrants, topped and tailed
2 sprigs fresh mint
1 tbsp clear honey
120ml/4fl oz apple juice
1tsp arrowroot or cornflour, mixed with 2 tbsp cold water
125g/4oz raspberries
225g/8oz strawberries, hulled and sliced

To decorate
mint leaves
a few sprigs of blackcurrant

1. Place the blackcurrants in a saucepan with the mint, honey and apple juice and slowly bring to simmering point. Simmer gently for 5 minutes – don't allow the fruit to overcook.
2. Remove from the heat and stir in the arrowroot or cornflour. Return to the heat and stir gently until the liquid thickens.
3. Remove from the heat and stir in the raspberries and strawberries. Allow to cool then chill until needed. Decorate with mint leaves and sprigs of currants before serving.

Nutrient	Units	per portion
Energy	Kcals	68.07
Vitamin **A**	mcg	12.25
Carotene	mcg	73.35
Vitamin **C**	mg	168.48
Vitamin **E**	mg	0.52
Fibre	g	3.27
Polyunsaturates	g	0.00
Monounsaturates	g	0.17
Saturated fat	g	0.00

Pumpkin Pie
Serves 8

Pastry
175g/6oz wholemeal flour or half and half
wholemeal and unbleached
75g/3oz sunflower spread with added vitamin E
approx 4tbsp skimmed milk

Filling
450g/1lb pumpkin or other squash
2 free-range eggs
4tbsp single cream
2tbsp honey
freshly grated nutmeg

1. Preheat the oven to 190°C/375F°/Gas Mark 5 and lightly oil a 20cm/8in flan dish or ring.
2. Sift the flour into a mixing bowl and rub in the fat until the mixture resembles breadcrumbs in consistency. Mix to a soft dough with the milk and roll out on a lightly floured surface. Line the flan ring with the pastry and prick the base of the pastry case.
3. Peel and chop the pumpkin and steam, boil or microwave in a minimum of water until cooked. Drain and purée in a food processor or blender.
4. Beat in the eggs, cream and honey and pour into the prepared pastry case. Grate the nutmeg over the top of the pie and bake for 25–30 minutes or until the custard is set.

Nutrient	Units	per portion
Energy	Kcals	188.11
Vitamin A	mcg	177.97
Carotene	mcg	332.96
Vitamin C	mg	8.01
Vitamin E	mg	4.65
Fibre	g	2.53
Polyunsaturates	g	3.45
Monounsaturates	g	4.49
Saturated fat	g	2.70

Red Fruit Salad
Serves 4

225g/8oz strawberries, hulled and halved
125g/4oz raspberries
225g/8oz red cherries, stoned
1.2kg/2½lb slice watermelon

1. Lightly toss the strawberries, raspberries and cherries in a bowl.
2. Using a Parisienne cutter (baller) scoop out balls of watermelon flesh. Add the balls, and any juice you collect, to the fruit salad.
3. Cut out the part of flesh that contains most of the pips and place in a sieve. Press the flesh through the sieve and pour the resulting juice into the fruit salad.

Nutrient	Units	per portion
Energy	Kcals	97.38
Vitamin A	mcg	68.95
Carotene	mcg	407.81
Vitamin C	mg	71.37
Vitamin E	mg	0.47
Fibre	g	1.94
Polyunsaturates	g	0.00
Monounsaturates	g	0.79
Saturated fat	g	0.00

Poached Fruit Salad
Serves 4

450g/1lb firm apricots, halved and stoned
450g/1lb firm peaches, halved and stoned
85ml/3fl oz peach syrup or similar fruit cordial
250ml/8fl oz water
1 ripe papaya, deseeded and cubed or sliced

1. Place the apricots and peaches in a stainless steel saucepan with the syrup and water. Bring to simmering point and cook for about 10 minutes until the fruit is soft but retains its shape. Remove from the heat.
2. When the fruit has cooled stir in the prepared papaya. Serve either at room temperature or chilled.

Nutrient	Units	per portion
Energy	Kcals	132.53
Vitamin **A**	mcg	232.88
Carotene	mcg	1392.75
Vitamin **C**	mg	104.62
Vitamin **E**	mg	0.00
Fibre	g	5.74
Polyunsaturates	g	0.00
Monounsaturates	g	0.34
Saturated fat	g	0.00

Eton Mess
Serves 4

Despite its name, a delicious dish!

1 small packet ratafia biscuits or macaroons (about 125g/4oz)
2 tbsp dry (fino) sherry
225g/8oz strawberries, hulled and sliced
175g/6oz raspberries
150ml/¼pt double cream
200g/7oz carton natural Greek yogurt

To decorate
reserved fruit from above
mint leaves
borage flowers (optional)

1. Cover the base of a serving dish with a layer of ratafia biscuits or crushed macaroons and spoon the sherry over them.
2. Arrange one-third of the strawberries and raspberries on top of the biscuits.

Nutrient	Units	per portion
Energy	Kcals	349.89
Vitamin **A**	mcg	266.04
Carotene	mcg	126.69
Vitamin **C**	mg	57.62
Vitamin **E**	mg	1.18
Fibre	g	2.09
Polyunsaturates	g	0.75
Monounsaturates	g	9.66
Saturated fat	g	15.18

3. Whip the cream until stiff and fold in the yogurt. Fold the rest of the fruit and biscuits into the cream, reserving some fruit for decorating the top. Spoon into the serving dish and decorate with fruit, mint leaves and borage flowers, if available.

Poached Apricots
Serves 4

450g/1lb ripe apricots, halved and stoned
4 tbsp peach syrup or cordial
scant 300ml/½pt water
1 cinnamon stick

1. Place the apricots in a saucepan with the remaining ingredients and simmer, very gently so that the fruit retains its shape, until the apricots are cooked – about 15 minutes.
2. Remove the cinnamon stick and allow the apricots to cool, then chill slightly before serving.

Nutrient	Units	per portion
Energy	Kcals	49.73
Vitamin **A**	mcg	70.88
Carotene	mcg	421.88
Vitamin **C**	mg	5.63
Vitamin **E**	mg	0.00
Fibre	g	1.80
Polyunsaturates	g	0.00
Monounsaturates	g	0.11
Saturated fat	g	0.00

Pears in Red Wine
Serves 4

6 firm or underripe dessert pears, peeled, halved and cored
50g/2oz demerara sugar
300 ml/½pt light red wine
300ml/½pt water
1 stick cinnamon, 3 cloves, 4 allspice berries, grating of nutmeg,
strip of orange peel, tied together in a muslin bag

Nutrient	Units	per portion
Energy	Kcals	165.50
Vitamin A	mcg	5.18
Carotene	mcg	31.50
Vitamin C	mg	9.00
Vitamin E	mg	0.00
Fibre	g	2.47
Polyunsaturates	g	0.00
Monounsaturates	g	0.22
Saturated fat	g	0.00

1. Place the pears in a saucepan with the remaining ingredients and simmer very gently so that the fruit retains its shape and does not overcook.
2. When the fruit is cooked (about 15 minutes, depending on the ripeness of the pears), remove from the pan. Boil the liquid to reduce it by half, then remove the muslin bag of spices.
3. Place the pears in a serving dish and pour over the reduced liquid. Chill before serving, or if preferred serve at room temperature.

Fruity Bread and Butter Pudding
Serves 6

4 slices bread, 2 white and 2 wholemeal, crusts removed
25g/1oz butter
75g/3oz mixed currants and raisins
4 dried apricots, chopped
2 free-range egg yolks
1 free-range egg
40g/1½oz muscovado sugar
½ tsp ground cinnamon
450ml/¾pt milk
½ tsp vanilla extract (not essence)

1. Spread the bread with the butter, cut into halves or quarters and arrange in an ovenproof dish, buttered side up.
2. Sprinkle the fruit over the top, pushing some down between and beneath the slices of bread.

162

3. Whisk the egg yolks, egg, sugar, cinnamon, milk and vanilla extract in a bowl and pour over the bread in the dish. Leave to stand for 30 minutes.
4. Preheat the oven to 190°C/375°F/Gas Mark 5. Place the pudding in a roasting pan of hot water and bake for about 40 minutes until the top is golden brown and the custard is set.

Nutrient	Units	per portion
Energy	Kcals	238.57
Vitamin **A**	mcg	137.52
Carotene	mcg	67.30
Vitamin **C**	mg	0.81
Vitamin **E**	mg	0.29
Fibre	g	1.48
Polyunsaturates	g	0.63
Monounsaturates	g	4.31
Saturated fat	g	5.02

Tricolour Melon Salad with Blackcurrant Coulis
Serves 8

For everyday use you can omit the kirsch and cassis, which are really for a special treat when entertaining.

1 honeydew melon
1 charentais melon
1 galia melon
2 tbsp kirsch (optional)
175g/6oz blackcurrants
1 tbsp clear honey or brown sugar (optional)
1 tbsp cassis (optional)

1. Prepare the melons by halving and discarding the seeds, then cut each melon in a different way to add to the interest of the salad – for example, use a melon baller (Parisienne cutter) on the honeydew, take small crescent-shaped slices from the galia and cube the charentais.
2. Toss the prepared melon in a bowl with the kirsch, if using. Cover and refrigerate until ready to serve.

3. Stew the blackcurrants in the minimum amount of water to prevent them burning. When soft, sieve the fruit and mix with the honey and cassis, if using. Chill before serving. Offer the blackcurrant coulis in a separate jug.

Nutrient	Units	per portion
Energy	Kcals	61.10
Vitamin A	mcg	82.28
Carotene	mcg	495.12
Vitamin C	mg	68.65
Vitamin E	mg	0.23
Fibre	g	1.87
Polyunsaturates	g	0.00
Monounsaturates	g	0.25
Saturated fat	g	0.00

Hot Fruit Salad

Serves 4

Make as much as you like because this is equally delicious for breakfast and will keep in the fridge for 5 days.

50g/2oz each of dried pears, peaches, apples,
apricots, prunes and raisins
stick of cinnamon
2 cloves
2 whole green cardamoms
juice of ½ lemon
2 tbsp brandy (optional)

Nutrient	Units	per portion
Energy	Kcals	179.95
Vitamin A	mcg	47.70
Carotene	mcg	288.48
Vitamin C	mg	1.92
Vitamin E	mg	0.11
Fibre	g	4.38
Polyunsaturates	g	0.01
Monounsaturates	g	0.37
Saturated fat	g	0.10

1. Place the ingredients in a saucepan and slowly bring to simmering point. Cook until the fruit is plump and softened.
2. Remove the cinnamon, cloves and cardomoms before serving.

Apple Strudel
Serves 6

75g/3oz wholemeal breadcrumbs
450g/1lb (about 2) Bramley apples
juice and zest of ½ lemon
25g/1oz sugar
4 allspice berries
4 cloves
1 cinnamon stick
2 tbsp water
75g/3oz raisins
75g/3oz walnut pieces
6 sheets of filo pastry or strudel leaves,
each measuring 30cm x 15cm/12 x 6in
25g/1oz unsalted butter, melted

1. Preheat the oven to 200°C/400°F/Gas Mark 6.
2. Toast the breadcrumbs either in the grill pan or by dry-frying in a heavy-based frying pan. Stir to cook evenly. Remove from the heat.
3. Peel and core the apples and cut the flesh into chunks. Place in a saucepan with the lemon juice and zest, sugar, spices and water. Cover and cook gently for about 3–4 minutes to soften and flavour the apple. Remove from the heat and remove the

Nutrient	Units	per portion
Energy	Kcals	241.43
Vitamin **A**	mcg	36.33
Carotene	mcg	30.48
Vitamin **C**	mg	8.82
Vitamin **E**	mg	0.44
Fibre	g	2.24
Polyunsaturates	g	6.20
Monounsaturates	g	3.33
Saturated fat	g	3.21

cinnamon stick, allspice berries and cloves. Stir in the raisins,walnut pieces and toasted breadcrumbs.

4. Place 4 sheets of pastry on top of each other, brushing with butter between layers, on a lightly oiled baking tray. Place the apple filling in the centre of the pastry, leaving about 4cm/1½in of pastry uncovered all the way round.

5. When all the filling is in place, lay 2 layers of pastry on top, brushing the top of each with melted butter. Tuck the edges of the bottom sheets of pastry up over the top ones to seal in the filling, brushing the area with butter to seal.

6. Brush the outside with the remaining butter and bake in the middle of the oven for about 15 minutes until golden brown. Slice into diamond shapes when cool.

Mango Fruit Terrine
Serves 8

400ml/14fl oz mango and apple juice, mango juice or orange juice
3 tsp powdered gelatine
150ml/¼pt boiling water
1 firm but ripe pear, diced
1 banana, sliced
1 mango, cubed
1 pink grapefruit, segmented
125g/4oz strawberries, hulled and halved

To decorate
fresh mint leaves
additional strawberries

Nutrient	Units	per portion
Energy	Kcals	93.40
Vitamin **A**	mcg	198.19
Carotene	mcg	1189.21
Vitamin **C**	mg	53.41
Vitamin **E**	mg	1.13
Fibre	g	2.68
Polyunsaturates	g	0.01
Monounsaturates	g	0.27
Saturated fat	g	0.02

1. Place the fruit juice in a basin. Sprinkle the gelatine onto the boiling water and stir until dissolved. Stir into the juice and allow to cool.
2. Pack the fruit into a 1.2 litre/2 pt terrine, loaf tin or fancy mould.
3. Pour over the cooled juice, which should be at setting point. Pack the fruit down into the juice.
4. Chill in the fridge for about 2 hours to allow it to set before serving.
5. To serve, either cut slices from the terrine tin or unmould and slice. Decorate with mint leaves and strawberries

Summer Sundae Terrine
Serves 4

Don't make this dessert too far ahead of serving as the ratafias will stay crisp in the mixture for only 1½–2 hours. However, it does need some chilling in the fridge before serving.

2 ripe peaches, peeled, stoned and sliced
175g/6oz raspberries
125g/4oz blueberries
125g/4oz redcurrants
about 50 ratafia biscuits (½ x 125g/4oz packet)
2 x 200g/7oz cartons natural Greek yogurt
2 tbsp clear honey

To decorate
sprigs of redcurrants
mint leaves
a few raspberries
borage flowers

Nutrient	Units	per portion
Energy	Kcals	243.66
Vitamin **A**	mcg	137.44
Carotene	mcg	133.78
Vitamin **C**	mg	46.35
Vitamin **E**	mg	1.63
Fibre	g	3.76
Polyunsaturates	g	0.26
Monounsaturates	g	4.54
Saturated fat	g	6.65

1. Place alternate layers of mixed fruit, ratafia biscuits and yogurt in individual sundae dishes or glasses, finishing with yogurt.
2. Spoon over the honey and leave it to seep through the yogurt and fruit while the dishes stand in the fridge.
3. Decorate as desired just before serving.

Fruity Rice Pudding
Serves 4

75g/3oz pudding (short-grain) rice
900ml/1½pt skimmed milk
4 whole green cardamoms
1 cinnamon stick
25g/1oz muscovado sugar
50g/2oz currants
50g/2oz raisins
4 dried apricots, chopped
½ mango, cubed (optional)
25g/1oz flaked almonds
freshly grated nutmeg
25g/1oz butter

1. Preheat the oven to 180°C/350°F/Gas Mark 4 and wash the rice.
2. Infuse the milk by heating with the cardamoms and cinnamon stick gently for 10 minutes.
3. Remove the cardamoms and cinnamon and add the rice. Simmer for 20 minutes, stirring often.

Nutrient	Units	per portion
Energy	Kcals	358.10
Vitamin **A**	mcg	216.05
Carotene	mcg	978.19
Vitamin **C**	mg	20.88
Vitamin **E**	mg	1.29
Fibre	g	2.83
Polyunsaturates	g	0.71
Monounsaturates	g	5.09
Saturated fat	g	3.76

4. Transfer the rice and milk to a 1.2 litre/2pt ovenproof dish. Stir in the sugar, currants, raisins, apricots and mango, if using, and cook in the oven for 30 minutes.
5. Remove from the oven, sprinkle the almonds and nutmeg on top and dot with the butter. Return to the oven for 15 minutes for a perfect, golden-brown pudding.

Panforte
Serves 15

Panforte is a Christmas speciality from Siena, Italy, which is eaten in small servings. Although panforte is traditionally round, I find it quicker and easier to work with rice paper in a square tin.

rice paper
125g/4oz toasted hazelnuts
125g/4oz toasted almonds
225g/8oz candied peel (orange, lemon and citron)
125g/4oz candied fruit
2 tsp ground cinnamon
½ tsp ground nutmeg
½ tsp ground cloves
125g/4oz unbleached white flour
125g/4oz clear honey
125g/4oz muscovado sugar
icing sugar (optional)

1. Preheat the oven to 150°C/300°F/Gas Mark 2 and place a layer of rice paper in a 20cm/8in square tin. Put strips around the sides as well.

Nutrient	Units	per portion
Energy	Kcals	208.25
Vitamin **A**	mcg	0.41
Carotene	mcg	2.39
Vitamin **C**	mg	0.00
Vitamin **E**	mg	1.97
Fibre	g	1.33
Polyunsaturates	g	1.15
Monounsaturates	g	6.34
Saturated fat	g	0.60

2. Chop the nuts, peel and fruit and mix with the spices and flour.
3. Heat the honey and sugar until they melt together. Stir into the dry ingredients to make a sticky mass.
4. Put the fruit mixture into the tin and either cover with another layer of rice paper, pressing down lightly, or press and flatten the mixture leaving it uncovered. Bake for 30 minutes.
5. Remove from the oven and cool in the tin. When removed, sprinkle the top of the uncovered version with sifted icing sugar. When cool, store in an airtight container. It will keep for 1 month.

Dried Fruit Petits Fours
Makes 12

50g/2oz ground hazelnuts
125g/4oz dried fruit (e.g. apricots, dates, figs)
pinch of ground mixed spice
1 tbsp clear honey
desiccated coconut, drinking chocolate
or cocoa powder, to decorate

1. Place the nuts in a food processor together with the dried fruit, spice and honey. Process to a sticky consistency.
2. Roll small walnut-sized balls of the mixture in desiccated coconut, cocoa powder or drinking chocolate.
3. Place in petit four papercases. Store in an airtight tin for up to 2 weeks.

Nutrient	Units	per portion
Energy	Kcals	54.22
Vitamin A	mcg	0.13
Carotene	mcg	0.75
Vitamin C	mg	0.00
Vitamin E	mg	0.62
Fibre	g	0.45
Polyunsaturates	g	0.27
Monounsaturates	g	2.22
Saturated fat	g	0.19

Baking

Apple and Blackberry Pie
Serves 6

Pastry
75g/3oz wholemeal flour
75g/3oz plain unbleached flour
1tsp baking powder
2 tbsp oat bran
75g/3oz sunflower spread with added vitamin E
2–3 tbsp water
1tsp sesame seeds

Filling
450g/1lb dessert apples, peeled, cored and sliced
225g/8oz blackberries
3 tbsp clear honey

Nutrient	Units	per portion
Energy	Kcals	267.29
Vitamin **A**	mcg	119.26
Carotene	mcg	135.05
Vitamin **C**	mg	8.63
Vitamin **E**	mg	6.40
Fibre	g	4.02
Polyunsaturates	g	4.64
Monounsaturates	g	4.31
Saturated fat	g	1.95

1. Preheat the oven to 200°C/400°F/Gas Mark 6.
2. Place the flours, baking powder and oat bran in a bowl. Rub in the fat until the mixture resembles breadcrumbs. Gradually add the water and mix to a firm dough.
3. Mix the apples and blackberries together then place in a 900ml/1½pt pie dish and drizzle over the honey or sugar.
4. Turn the dough onto a floured surface and knead lightly. Roll out thinly to a round about 5cm/2in larger than the pie dish.

5. Cut off a narrow strip all round and use to cover the dampened rim of the pie dish, then brush with water.
6. Lift the pastry onto a rolling pin and place over the fruit, sealing the edges well. Trim and flute the edges and make a hole in the centre. Brush with water and sprinkle the pie with the sesame seeds.
7. Bake for 30–40 minutes. Serve hot or cold.

Date and Walnut Cake
Serves 8

125g/4oz sunflower spread with added vitamin E
125g/4oz dark muscovado sugar
2 free-range eggs, lightly beaten
125g/4oz dates, pitted and chopped
50g/2oz walnut pieces
150g/5oz wholemeal flour, sifted, or Granary flour
pinch of baking powder

1. Preheat the oven to 190°C/375°F/Gas Mark 5 and line a 450g/1lb loaf tin with greaseproof paper
2. Cream together the fat and sugar. Beat in the eggs, alternating with a little flour if the mixture looks like curdling.
3. Fold in the fruit, walnuts, flour and baking powder and spoon into the prepared tin. Bake for 40 minutes until golden brown and an inserted skewer comes out clean.

Nutrient	Units	per portion
Energy	Kcals	331.75
Vitamin A	mcg	167.80
Carotene	mcg	123.44
Vitamin C	mg	0.00
Vitamin E	mg	6.59
Fibre	g	2.53
Polyunsaturates	g	8.40
Monounsaturates	g	6.40
Saturated fat	g	3.13

Carrot Cake
Serves 10

2 free-range eggs
125g/4oz dark muscovado sugar
85ml/3fl oz sunflower oil with added vitamin E
175g/6oz carrots, grated
125g/4oz wholemeal flour
1 tsp baking powder
1 tsp ground cinnamon
½ tsp ground nutmeg
50g/2oz walnuts, chopped
50g/2oz raisins

Frosting (optional)
50g/2oz butter
1tbsp honey
50g/2oz icing sugar
1tsp Culpeper sweet orange oil

1. Preheat the oven to 190°C/375°F/Gas Mark 5 and lightly oil an 18cm/7in cake tin.
2. Whisk the eggs and sugar until thick and creamy. Whisk in the sunflower oil .
3. Fold in the rest of the ingredients and pour into the prepared cake tin. Bake for 30 minutes or until an inserted skewer comes out clean.
4. When the cake is completely cold top with frosting, if desired.

Nutrient	Units	per portion
Energy	Kcals	261.90
Vitamin **A**	mcg	285.94
Carotene	mcg	1345.66
Vitamin **C**	mg	0.40
Vitamin **E**	mg	4.82
Fibre	g	1.61
Polyunsaturates	g	5.74
Monounsaturates	g	5.63
Saturated fat	g	4.20

Orange Syrup Cake
Serves 8

175g/6oz muscovado sugar
175g/6oz sunflower spread with added vitamin E
50g/2oz candied orange peel, finely chopped
3 free-range eggs, beaten
4 tbsp orange juice
275g/9 oz fine semolina
3 tsp baking powder
50g/2oz ground almonds
50g/2oz fine oatmeal

Syrup
4 tbsp clear honey
4 tbsp water
juice of 1 lemon
juice of 1 orange

1. Preheat the oven to 190°C/375°F/Gas Mark 5 and lightly oil a 20cm/8in cake tin.
2. Cream the sugar and fat until it reaches a soft, dropping consistency then stir in the orange peel. Carefully and slowly beat in the eggs and orange juice.
3. Beat in the semolina, baking powder, almonds and oatmeal. Place the mixture in the tin and bake for 35 minutes or until an inserted skewer comes out clean and the top is golden brown. Protect the top from over-browning by covering with a piece of foil or greaseproof paper during the last stages of cooking. Remove from the oven and place on a wire rack to cool.

Nutrient	Units	per portion
Energy	Kcals	501.77
Vitamin A	mcg	236.59
Carotene	mcg	167.24
Vitamin C	mg	6.51
Vitamin E	mg	10.17
Fibre	g	1.68
Polyunsaturates	g	8.51
Monounsaturates	g	10.63
Saturated fat	g	4.16

4. Heat the syrup ingredients together until the honey has melted. Pierce the hot cake all over with the skewer and slowly pour the syrup over so that it is absorbed into the cake. Leave to become completely cold before serving.

Australian Fig Cake
Serves 12

450g/1lb dried figs, or half figs and half dried apricots
125g/4oz sunflower spread with added vitamin E
175g/6oz brown sugar
2 free-range eggs
200g/7oz wholemeal flour
1tsp baking powder
½ tsp ground cinnamon
½ tsp ground cloves
120ml/4fl oz skimmed milk
75g/3oz walnut pieces
75g/3oz raisins
glace figs, to decorate (optional)

1. Preheat the oven to 190°C/375°F/Gas Mark 5 and lightly oil a 20cm/8in cake tin.
2. Stew the fruit in enough water to cover for about 15 minutes, being careful not to let it burn. Remove from the heat, strain and set aside to cool, reserving the cooking liquid.

Nutrient	Units	per portion
Energy	Kcals	328.98
Vitamin **A**	mcg	96.85
Carotene	mcg	87.77
Vitamin **C**	mg	0.54
Vitamin **E**	mg	3.74
Fibre	g	4.66
Polyunsaturates	g	5.98
Monounsaturates	g	4.20
Saturated fat	g	2.37

3. Cream the fat and sugar to a soft dropping consistency. Beat in the eggs.
4. Sift the flour, baking powder and spices into a mixing bowl, adding the bran left in the sieve to the bowl.
5. Fold the flour into the creamed ingredients alternately with the milk and 1–2 tbsp of the liquid from the stewed fruit.
6. Chop the stewed figs and fold them into the mixture with the walnuts and raisins.
7. Spoon into the prepared tin and bake for 1 hour 15 minutes or until an inserted skewer comes out clean. Remove and allow to cool in the tin for about 15 minutes before turning out onto a wire rack. When completely cold store in an airtight container for up to 2 weeks.

Raisin Bread

This bread is delicious for breakfast.

300ml/½pt skimmed milk
1 tbsp honey
1 tbsp vegetable oil
25g/1oz fresh yeast or 2 tsp dried yeast
225g/8oz wholemeal flour
225g/8oz unbleached white flour
pinch of salt
1 tsp ground cinnamon
175g/6oz raisins
1 egg, beaten

1. Warm the milk to blood heat (warm but not hot when you dip in a finger) and remove from the heat. Stir in the honey and oil and crumble the yeast over, stirring well until the yeast is dissolved.
2. Sift the flour into a bowl, adding the bran left in the sieve to the bowl. Stir in the salt, cinnamon and raisins, ensuring the raisins do not stick together in clumps.
3. Pour the yeast liquid onto the dry ingredients and combine to make a soft dough. Lightly flour the work surface and knead for about 5 minutes until smooth and no longer sticky.

4. Return the dough to the bowl and cover the top to prevent it drying out. Stand in a warm place until doubled in size – about 1 hour.

5. Preheat the oven to 200°C/400°F/Gas Mark 6 and lightly oil a 1kg/2lb loaf tin.

6. Turn the dough out onto the work surface again and 'knock back' (knead out the air). Shape and place in the tin. Cover and leave to rise for about 40 minutes until the dough is to the top of the tin.

7. Brush the top with beaten egg and bake for 30–35 minutes until golden brown and the loaf sounds hollow when tapped on the base.

QUICK RISING TIP

Instead of leaving the dough to rise (step 4) it may be placed in a microwave-proof container, covered and put in the microwave on full power for 10 seconds, then rested for 10 minutes. Repeat and the dough will have doubled in size. Continue as outlined in the rest of the recipe.

Nutrient	Units	per loaf
Energy	Kcals	2254.34
Vitamin A	mcg	7.28
Carotene	mcg	25.65
Vitamin C	mg	4.75
Vitamin E	mg	6.73
Fibre	g	30.73
Polyunsaturates	g	10.97
Monounsaturates	g	9.39
Saturated fat	g	3.71

Granola

2 tbsp clear honey
2 tbsp sunflower oil with added vitamin E
225g/8oz porridge oats
50g/2oz flaked or desiccated coconut
50g/2oz whole or chopped hazelnuts
50g/2oz sesame seeds
125g/4oz raisins

1. Preheat the oven to 180°C/350°F/Gas Mark 4 and lightly oil a large roasting tin or ovenproof dish.
2. Warm the honey gently and stir in the oil.
3. Place all the dry ingredients except the raisins in a large bowl. Add the honey and oil and mix thoroughly until the dry ingredients are coated.
4. Spread the mixture over the base of the tin and bake for about 20 minutes until golden brown. Stir the mixture halfway through cooking to ensure even cooking.
5. When completely cold stir in the raisins and store in an airtight container for up to 1 month.

HONEY TIP

The easiest way to measure honey and other viscous liquids is to place the jar or container on the scales and spoon out the amount required.

Nutrient	Units	per batch
Energy	Kcals	2286.73
Vitamin A	mcg	2.50
Carotene	mcg	15.00
Vitamin C	mg	2.50
Vitamin E	mg	33.13
Fibre	g	28.15
Polyunsaturates	g	35.57
Monounsaturates	g	56.33
Saturated fat	g	28.81

Glossary and abbreviations

Antioxidant A substance that delays or prevents oxidation. Oxidation makes butter go rancid and metal go rusty. For humans, too, there's no escape from free-radicals produced by oxidation, because they are a by-product of normal cell life (i.e respiration, or the burning of oxygen). It has been said free radicals are the price we have to pay for using oxygen.

ACE nutrients Nutrients with antioxidant powers include vitamins C, E and beta carotene, probably other carotenoids, and minerals such as zinc, selenium, copper and manganese. There are others and probably some yet to be discovered.

Carcinogens Substances that initiate or promote cancer.

Carotenoids Pigments ranging in colour from red through orange to yellow that are found in plant foods, insects, birds and other plant-eating animals, including humans. There are more than 650 carotenoids, many of which are active antioxidants. Beta carotene has the highest activity and is the most widely available.

Catalase Antioxidant enzyme that occurs naturally in the human body. It contains iron and catalyses (brings about by its presence) the decomposition of hydrogen peroxide.

DNA Deoxyribonucleic acid, the genetic material found in the nucleus (centre) of the cell and consisting of coiled strands of 46 chromosomes in 23 pairs.

DRV (also EAR/LRNI/RNI) British government standards – Dietary Reference Values – for how much of each vitamin and mineral it is thought we need (see Appendix 1).

Free radical A highly reactive molecule made inside the body and encountered from outside pollutants. Free-radical molecules are one electron short (electrons are usually paired), so they grab an electron from another molecule, disturbing the chemical balance by making another electron a single unit, thus setting up a chain reaction. Free radicals are produced constantly in the body as part of normal functions. They need to be dealt with immediately because they can damage DNA.

Glutathione An antioxidant produced naturally in the body. It is essential for the production of several protective enzymes. It is a scavenger of hydroxyl radicals and singlet oxygen.

Glutathione peroxidase An antioxidant enzyme found in the human body containing selenium and important in the decomposition of hydrogen peroxide and lipid peroxides.

Hydrogen peroxide A highly reactive molecule that can cause tissue damage. It is not a free radical.

Mineral Inorganic substance needed for normal function of the body (e.g. calcium). Trace elements are minerals required in minute amounts (e.g. zinc).

Oxidation The process in which oxygen is combined with other substances. When another molecule is oxidized it may go on to produce free radicals. Oxidation therefore increases the demand for antioxidants.

Oxidative stress A condition in which free radicals are formed in excess of the body's ability to remove them, resulting in damage to body cells and tissues.

Singlet oxygen An active form of oxygen that can lead to free-radical formation and may also be generated by free-radical reactions.

Superoxide A highly reactive form of oxygen produced when oxygen is reduced by one electron. Superoxide is produced during normal body functions, and has the potential to produce free radicals unless it is destroyed by the enzyme superoxide dismutase.

Superoxide dismutase An antioxidant enzyme found naturally in body cells. One form of the enzyme contains manganese and another contains copper and zinc.

Vitamin Organic substance needed in small amounts for growth and in normal daily chemistry of the body. It is essential to eat vitamins in food because the body cannot make vitamins (with the exception of vitamin D made by the action of sunlight on the skin and vitamins B12 and K_2 made by intestinal bacteria) .

Abbreviations

g = gram

mg = milligram or one thousandth of 1 gram

mcg = microgram or one millionth of 1 gram

Appendix I

There are British government standards for how much of certain vitamins and minerals it is thought we need. These are called **Dietary Reference Values**. There are several categories.

EAR (Estimated Average Requirement) Because we are all different standards have been set for average needs, recognizing that some people need more and some less.

RNI (Reference Nutrient Intake) The amount that is enough for virtually everyone, including those with high requirements. The RNI is higher than most people need, so anyone eating that much of a nutrient is unlikely to be deficient.

LRNI (Lower Reference Nutrient Intake) the amount needed by those with low needs. If people habitually eat less than the LRNI they are highly likely to be deficient in nutrients.

Safe Intake Where the government's expert panel which set the DRVs felt there was not enough information to estimate EARs, RNIs or LRNIs they set a safe intake which is one judged to be sufficient for most people's needs, but not so large as to cause undesirable effects.

What the British DRV report says about ACE nutrients

Beta carotene

There is neither an EAR nor RNI for beta-carotene or any of the other carotenoids. The DRV report says:

'It has been suggested that they (carotenoids) act as antioxidants in tissues, deactivating free radicals and excited oxygen, and specifically that a high dietary intake of carotenoids confers some protection against cancer. There is an inverse relationship between the incidence of some cancers and the consumption of fruit and vegetables (many of which contain carotenoids), but there is no proof that carotenoids are the protective factor... The Panel considered the evidence too insufficient to make any specific recommendations about the consumption of carotenoids beyond that needed to supply vitamin A.'

Even though the British government has not yet recognized beta carotene as an essential nutrient, some scientists have calculated what they think is an optimal level, i.e the amount needed to give you protection against disease, rather than the DRV amounts which are designed to be sufficient to prevent deficiencies.

The average British intake of beta carotene is 2.4mg/day for men and 2.1 mg/day for women.

Vitamin A

This is not considered to be an antioxidant but it does have a related role. It comes as retinol in foods of animal origin, or as beta carotene in plant foods which is converted to retinol in the body. In the table below 6mcg of beta carotene is the equivalent of 1mcg of retinol

DRVs for Vitamin A mcg (microgram or one-millionth of 1g) retinol equivalent per day				
Age	LRNI	EAR	RNI	Food sources
0–12 months	150	250	350 =	600g (approx 1pt) of breast milk
1–3 years	200	300	400 =	25g/1oz carrots
4–6 years	200	300	400 =	50g/2oz spinach
7–0 years	250	350	500 =	125g/4oz cheddar + 25g/1oz carrots
11–14 years	250	400	600 =	75g/3oz red pepper or 200g/7oz tomatoes

	Males	Females	Males	Females	Males	Females
15-50 years	300	250	500	400	700	600
Pregnant women	+ 100					
Lactating women	+ 350					

The average British intake of vitamin A is 1277mcg/day for men and 1133mcg/d for women.

Intakes of retinol (vitamin A) in excess of need, if taken over a long period of time, may be dangerous, leading to liver and bone damage and other problems. Regular intakes should not exceed 7500 mcg/day for women and 9000mcg/d for men. An intake of retinol in excess of 3300 mcg/day for pregnant women may cause birth defects (see Chapter 6, page 103).

Vitamin E (alpha-tocopherol)

The amount of vitamin E you need depends on how much polyunsaturated fat you eat. It's thought that for every gram of polyunsaturated fat eaten, 0.4mg of vitamin E is needed. However, EC Labelling Directives have set an RDA of 10mg vitamin E a day. Compilers of the DRV report felt it was not possible to set DRVs for vitamin E, but safe intakes were set at more than 4mg a day for men and more than 3mg a day for women. Yet, it says few adverse effects have been reported from doses of vitamin E up to 3200mg a day.

Some foods high in polyunsaturates, such as some sunflower spreads, have vitamin E already added.

Vitamin C

The British government's Dietary Reference Values report says vitamin C is an important antioxidant. and it bases estimates of need on how much is required for an minimal body pool of 25mg a day. It says 'Claims that vitamin C can prevent tissue damage are still being assessed.'

Dietary Reference Values for Vitamin C mg/day

Age	LRNI	EAR	RNI	Food sources
0–12 months	6	15	25 =	675g (just over 1pt) breast milk
1–10 years	8	20	30 =	100g (small glass) orange juice
11–14 years	9	22	35 =	half an orange
15 years +	10	25	40 =	71g/2½oz strawberries
Additional amounts to be added to pre-pregnancy DRVs				
Pregnant women + 10				
Lactating women + 30				

The average British intake of vitamin C is 74.6mg/day for men and 73.1mg/day for women.

Zinc

British DRVs for zinc don't specify any antioxidant requirements, although they have been calculated bearing in mind that zinc is involved in several enzyme systems, and it is as an enzyme that zinc is active as an antioxidant.

DRVs for zinc mg/day				
Age	LRNI	EAR	RNI	Food sources
0-6 months	2.6	3.3	4 =	1400g (2pt) breast milk
7 months–3yrs	3	3.8	5 =	64g/2¼oz stewed liver
4–6 years	4	5	6.5 =	just over 125g/4oz lean lamb
7–10 years	4	5.4	7 =	portion fortified breakfast cereal
11–14 years	5.3	7	9 =	round wholemeal sardine sandwiches + 300ml/½pt milk + main meal of lean meat and green veg
	Males Females		Males Females	Males Females
15 years+	5.5 4		7.3 5.5	9.5 7

The average British intake for zinc is 11.4mg/day for men and 8.4mg/day for women.

Copper

There was only a small amount of information about the need for copper so only RNIs were set

DRVs for Copper mg/day

Age	RNI	Food sources
0–12 months	0.3 =	babies born with reserves
1–3 years	0.4 =	50g/2 oz cod + 50g/2oz peas
4–6 years	0.6 =	50g/2oz cooked pulses (lentils) + portion porridge
7–10 years	0.7 =	50g/2 oz hazel nuts
11–14 years	0.8 =	50g/ 2oz prawns
15–16 years	1 =	wholemeal or rye bread peanut butter sandwiches + 25g/1 oz shellfish
18 + years	1.2 =	25g/1oz crab meat

Additional amounts needed for conception and in pregnancy are thought to be fulfilled by the mother's adaptive responses

Lactating women + 0.3

The average British intake for copper is 1.63mg/day for men and 1.23mg/d for women.

Selenium

The DRV panel recognized that selenium is part of an enzyme that gives antioxidant protection. However, it said there was no evidence that selenium helped prevent cancer, or that smoking and oral contraceptives increased selenium requirements. There was not enough information to set EARs. The upper intake for selenium has been set at 6mcg per kilogram of body weight a day for adults.

DRVs for Selenium mcg/day

Age	LRNI	RNI	Food sources	
0–3 months	4	10 = no figures for breast milk		
4–6 months	5	13 = 50g/2oz cereal + 50g/2 oz milk		
7–9 months	5	10 = 1 egg = 6.6mcg		
10–12 months	6	10		
1–3 years	7	15 = 100g/3½ oz lean pork		
4–6 years	10	20 = 75g/3oz lamb's liver		
7–10 years	16	30 = 75g/3oz fish		
11–14 years	25	45 = 130g/4½oz liver		
	Males	*Females*	*Males*	*Females*
15–18 years	40	40	70	60
19 + years	40	40	75	60
Lactating women	+ 15		+ 15	

The average intake of selenium (an estimate for south-east England only) is 65mcg/day for both men and women.

Manganese

A safe intake has been set of more than 1.4mg a day for adults and 16 mcg per kg of body weight for infants and children. The average British intake of manganese is estimated to be 4.6mg/day per person.

EC recommendations

The EC has proposed a set of recommended intakes of vitamins and minerals, but this is also conservative in its estimate of the amounts we need, and again is based on preventing deficiency diseases rather than achieving protection against ill health.

Like the British government's DRVs, the EC has a set of three figures:

Lowest threshold intake (LTI), an intake below which almost all individuals will get sick;
Average requirement (AR), which speaks for itself
Population reference intake (PRI), an intake that meets the needs of virtually everyone, corresponding to the British RNIs.

Summary of the Nutrient Intakes for the EC (ACE nutrients only)

Amounts per day for adults (where figures for women are different they are expressed in brackets).

Nutrient	Average requirement	Population intake reference	Lowest threshold intake
Vitamin A (mcg)	500 (400)	700 (600)	300 (250)
Folate (mcg)	140	200	85
Vitamin C (mg)	30	45	12
Vitamin E (mg)	—	0.4 for every gram of polyunsaturated fat eaten	4 (3) regardless of polyunsaturated fat intake
Zinc (mg)	7.5 (5.5)	9.5 (7)	5.5 (4)
Copper (mg)	0.8	1.1	0.6
Selenium (mcg)	100	130	70

Safe intakes were also given for manganese at 1–10mg/day. There was no recommendation for beta carotene. However, EC Labelling Directives set an RDA of 10mg vitamin E a day.

Appendix II

Healthy Diet – Two Summaries

World Health Organisation's Population Goals		
	Limits for population average intakes, as % of daily energy/calorie intake	
	Lower limit	Upper limit
Total fat	15	**30**
Saturated	0	**10**
Polyunsaturated	**3**	**7**
Dietary cholesterol	0mg/day	300mg/day
Total carbohydrate	**55**	75
Complex carbohydrates	**50**	70
Total dietary fibre	**27g/day**	40g/day
Free sugars	0	**10**
Salt	—	**6g/day**

Diet, nutrition and the prevention of chronic diseases, World Health Organisation 1990

Figures in bold are the ones that as a nation we should try to achieve

Fibre options
It may look as though the World Health Organisation and the British Dietary Reference Values overleaf are recommending different fibre intakes, but in fact they are very similar. It's just that WHO measures total dietary fibre and the DRVs go for the more precise measure of non-starch polysaccharides, the fibre constituent of plants. The lower intake recommendation of the WHO (27g/day total dietary fibre) 'translates' into 24g/day NSP, which is the maximum recommended amount recommended by the DRVs. The discrepancy here can probably be explained because the WHO is making worldwide recommendations and in some under-developed countries the fibre intake is much higher (40g/day total

dietary fibre or 36g/day NSP). The WHO does not want people to move away from their traditional diets towards the Western diet with all its health-related problems.ACE nutrients 11, 179

British dietary reference values – a summary

	Percentage daily total energy/calorie intake		
	Individual minimum	Population average	Individual maximum
Total fat		33 (35)	
Saturated fat		10 (11)	
Polyunsaturates		* 6 (6.5)	10
n–3 0.2			
n–6 1.0			
Monounsaturates		12 (13)	
**Trans fatty acids		2 (2)	
Total carbohydrate		47 (50)	
Free sugars	0	10 (11)	
Fibre (non-starch polysaccharides)	12g/day	18g/day	24g/day

The figures in brackets are for those people who do not drink alcohol which on average accounts for 5 per cent of food intake.

Protein is not mentioned, but it accounts for about 15 per cent of calories in Britain. This is more than is needed but the British experts say it is not necessary to eat less as at that level it doesn't appear to do you any harm.

* Polyunsaturates are divided into two types: n–3 (omega 3) and n–6 (omega 6). Omega 3 type are found in fish and green leafy vegetables. Omega 6 are found in seeds and plants, the main British dietary sources being sunflower oil, corn oil and the other vegetable oils. Minimum levels have been set because it's essential they are eaten.

** Trans fatty acids. The British line is not to eat more than we currently do – about 5g a day on average, or 2 per cent of total calories. That means not increasing the amount of cakes, biscuits, meat products and milk products that contain hydrogenated fats. It is the process of hydrogenation (hardening) of fats to make them more stable and increase the shelf-life of foods that has led to an increase in trans fatty acid intake. Interest in trans fatty acids has grown because it's been suggested they may be linked to heart disease in the same way as saturated fat.

Index